the gifts of grief

the gifts of grief

FINDING LIGHT IN THE DARKNESS OF LOSS

THERÈSE AMRHEIN TAPPOUNI

Hierophant publishing

Cover design by Kathryn Sky-Peck
Cover art by © iStockphoto.com/Phillip Jones
Text design by Jane Hagaman

Hierophant Publishing
8301 Broadway, Suite 219
San Antonio, TX 78209
888-800-4240
www.hierophantpublishing.com

If you are unable to order this book from your local
bookseller, you may order directly from the publisher.

Library of Congress Control Number: 2013930164

ISBN 978-1-938289-09-5

10 9 8 7 6 5 4 3 2 1

Printed on acid-free paper in the United States

This book is dedicated in admiration and love to the courageous . . . you who are willing to look for the light, shine it on your journey, and begin anew. May you find the gifts that await you and receive the peace you've earned as you journey into the darkness of your loss.

There is a crack, a crack in everything.
That's how the light gets in.

—Leonard Cohen, "Anthem"

Contents

Acknowledgments

I am so blessed with the presence in my life of my partner and editor, Lance Ware, for his critical eye, loving support, and meticulous editing throughout the creation of this book. I thank my children, whose loving belief in my work and life, and their own passionate gifts to the world, are an unending source of my heart's gratitude.

Special thanks to the professional and patient folks at Hierophant Publishing, especially Randy Davila, who encouraged this work, Allison Jacobs, who is always there for questions and support, and the team who made this book more beautiful than I would have imagined possible.

To Michael Hoppé, whose music inspires me, and Jean Houston, my inspirational teacher, who introduced me to the hero/heroine's journey many years ago. I have been given many gifts.

Introduction

The most beautiful people are those who have known defeat,
known suffering, known struggle, known loss, and have found
their way out of the depths. These persons have an appreciation, a sensitivity, and an understanding of life that fills them
with compassion, gentleness, and a deep loving concern.

—Elisabeth Kübler-Ross

My son died in July 1974, the summer before his twelfth
birthday. I had no forewarning, no sense that my life,
and that of our family, would be divided into chapters: Before
Michael, and After Michael. I was peeling potatoes late that
afternoon. My son Christopher, then four years old, and my
daughter Mary, nearly three, were a few feet from me watching *Sesame Street*. Someone banged on the front door, and as I
opened it, wiping my hands on my apron, I saw the frantic face
of Michael's closest friend. He and Michael had left the house
a short time before, riding their bikes to swim practice. Time
froze. I never knew what that meant before. Everything around

me slowed, like a movie that just stops and leaves the audience sitting in the dark. I didn't want the movie to resume. Whatever it was he was about to say, I knew my life had changed forever.

I don't remember getting to the scene, but I remember my thirteen-year-old daughter, Michelle, standing nearby with her friends, her horrified eyes fixed on her brother lying in the street. Two women were sitting by him, holding his hands. Off to the side, a delivery van angled into the ditch, the driver sobbing. The cookies and crackers painted on the truck's panels were garishly bright. Michael's mangled bicycle lay near the side of the road.

As I knelt by my son in the blistering hot street that day, a cone of silence held Michael and me, muffling the crying of those standing close by. For a brief time, I was lifted above the scene, seeing all of the players and refusing to be one of them. And then I fell to Earth. My heart broke open, pure terror spilled into my bloodstream, and chills of dread washed through my body. I tried to force time to retreat, go back. Please, let this be a dream, let me be standing by the stove serving dinner onto the white plates, with everyone accounted for at the table. Then the awful vibration of sirens broke through, shattering the silence and the connection. Michael's eyes closed. Even as paramedics lifted my son into the ambulance and led me to the front seat, I heard the sirens as if they were coming for and taking away someone else.

For ten days our son lay in a coma in the intensive care unit. His father and I waited daily for our two brief visits, but my spirit hovered in that room every waking moment. Sometimes other family joined us, and twice I gave away my precious time to others—once to my husband's aunt, who wanted to sprinkle Michael with water she'd brought from the shrine at Lourdes, and the other to my sister. When it was our turn, we washed our hands and walked like zombies into the buzzing, whirring atmosphere of the ICU.

While we waited for hours on end to catch sight of a doctor, my body existed at a basic level. Other than constant trips to the bathroom and nothing to eat but oatmeal, my life revolved around that bed in the ICU, the wheezing of the machines, the coldness of the hospital mattress my son lay on. The doctors' absence was purposeful: they had no hope for Michael's recovery and dreaded meeting with parents who had this particular pleading look of *please give me good news*. They were trained to tamp down their feelings so they wouldn't burn out.

I'll never forget one neurosurgeon telling me he had become emotionally involved in Michael's case. While taking communion at his church, not our family's church, the priest leaned over, placed the wafer on his tongue, and said to him: "Take care of Michael Tappouni." Maybe it was because he was in a sacred space, but his heart cracked open and he saw my son as a person, not a statistical brain injury. It didn't change the outcome, but it did change the energy surrounding Michael's care.[1]

I was fortunate to have a supportive family—particularly my sisters, who left their busy lives to keep the house running and look after our five children aged thirteen to three as their father, Michael, and I disappeared. Every day I awoke thinking it was a nightmare. This magical thinking is normal, but it caused even more pain as I was forced to realize the reality of our situation daily. Michael never regained consciousness, and he slipped away quietly hours after the doctor removed his ventilator.

It had been raining all that morning, but suddenly the birds were singing, and the Florida green that hurts the eyes shimmered outside the window. When we left the hospital after signing papers that were a total blur, I was stunned at the beauty of the day and the music trailing out the windows of a car. How was it possible that music still played? That people continued on their errands, not knowing there had been a shift in the universe?

All of these emotions, all of these fears, prayers, and bargaining with God become part of our cells. These experiences influence how we react to our lives in a very specific way, for the rest of our lives.

---

1 New research in physics and biology is showing the important relationships of the energy surrounding people, including the ability of caretakers to affect those being cared for in a positive or negative way.

The Gifts of Grief

Some of you can relate to my story. You, too, have had a loved one in the hospital and felt the frustration, pain, and hope of ICUs, waiting rooms, and medical jargon. Yet each of us experiences it all on a very individual level: with others surrounding you, or alone; with kind and supportive doctors, or busy and absent ones; with short stays, or long, difficult weeks or months. What matters is what medical and physical science now knows and teaches—all of these emotions, all of these fears, prayers, and bargaining with God, become part of our cells. These experiences influence how we react to our lives in a very specific way, for the rest of our lives. For me, grief and its devastating effects on individuals and families have been on my mind, or I should say, in my heart, since Michael's death.

After we buried Michael, his brothers and sisters required my presence in a way they hadn't before. The grief of siblings is complex and difficult, and an absent mom was not an option. I had to keep my outward grief hidden for private times, or so I thought. Like the rest of my family, I had no training in how to show grief in a healthy way. My tears were saved for my bedroom—and my closet.

⌒

Today, my heart is at peace. Though the scars are visible and the pain comes back at certain times, my heart no longer bleeds from the jagged cuts of grief. This was not true in July 1974, and it would not be true for many years to come. Following Michael's death, my husband and I became strangers in a strange world, as if we too had entered a coma. Another death, the death of our marriage, would follow many years later. This is a heartbreakingly foreseeable event for many couples who have lost children, though we managed to hold on for a long time. The divorce cascaded into the death of a family business and a numbing period of ill health.

Throughout, I struggled to model to my children that you can be beaten down by grief but choose to rise again, stronger and more compassionate than ever. I refused to be seen as a victim. I didn't want to be simply a survivor. But what else was there? I was never saintly. There were days when depression struck me down, when anger led me into a closet where I screamed at God in the darkness amidst the smell of mothballs and my dead child's clothing.

And yet I sensed a desire to grow through this achingly long winter of grief into someone else—someone expanded, not contracted by my grief. As I lay night after night waiting for sleep, I felt Michael's energy around me. Slowly I began to listen to my heart. Then one day in my meditation, I saw my heart and its possibilities. There, among the cracks and fissures, something luminous waited. I set out to determine the source of that light and recognized that I had to make a choice or I *would* fall into the trap of seeing myself as a victim. Michael, my other children, and I deserved more. Unfortunately, just making the choice wasn't enough. I couldn't bypass the dark night and go directly to the light. I had to participate in the entire journey before I could reach the grail.

To walk through grief is a heroic journey. No other challenge in life approaches it. Grief resembles a fire raging between us and our destination, and we cannot go around, over, or under it; we must go through it. This book is about facing that challenge we never wanted to take on. Throughout the journey I will bring you reassurance, guidance, and understanding.

To walk through grief is a heroic journey. No other challenge in life approaches it.

I am a licensed HeartMath® provider, a clinical hypnotherapist, a Somatic Intuitive Training™ practitioner, an author of six books, and a poet. None of these is as important as my experiences when I talk about grief to someone grieving. As someone who has been there, I'm equipped to offer you the gift of heart to support you in your process. My life allows me to say, I've been there. I know what it feels like. I promise you there is hope and healing, even from the most unthinkable grief.

I welcome you into this sacred space called the grieving process. You will always be safe in this place I've created through my heart's knowledge of grieving and my belief that our courage and ability to love are boundless. You will learn much about yourself—your strength and your beauty—within these pages. And you will never be alone.

The Gifts of Grief

Chapter 1

Courage—Taking the First Step

Sometimes in the stillness of the quiet, if we listen,
We can hear the whisper in the heart
Giving strength to weakness, courage to fear, hope to despair.

—Howard Thurman, *For the Inward Journey*

Some of you might have felt anger or resentment when you first saw the title of this book. Perhaps you even left it on the shelf for a time, saying it is impossible to find a gift in such agony. I understand. *The Gifts of Grief* title was chosen for those who are ready and willing to create a new path through life. Wendell Berry said, "It may be that when we no longer know what to do we have come to our real work and that when we no longer know which way to go we have begun our real journey." I believe that with all my heart, and I don't think there is a better definition of the opportunity present in grief than this one.

How to Read This Book

Think of this book and your grief as a journey—a journey remarkably like Dorothy's in *The Wizard of Oz*. Life is going along when suddenly, out of nowhere, a tornado touches down and moves you, violently, to a whole new world—the world of grief. Grief resembles a natural disaster, either one that has been accumulating around you, or one that strikes out of the blue and changes everything. This book is a guide through the steps of your journey through grief and into your new life. There is no timetable, and there are no rigid directions. *The Gifts of Grief* is a process. Your courage, the allies you surround yourself with, and the guidance in these pages will help you find your heart, your compassion, and the intelligence that leads you to your inner strength and, finally, healing.

Like Dorothy, you will have challenges, detours, disappointments, and epiphanies. Take the time you need, not what others suggest is the correct amount. Your journey is as individual as your fingerprints. The only thing I ask of you is that you follow the path from beginning to end—your new beginning—doing the exercises along the way, meditating, and always, always,

always recording your journey in a journal. If you feel the need to double back and revisit a certain section, or repeat a section over and over, it is your choice and your intuition that matter. The exercises are meant to be used repeatedly, and retracing your steps often reveals truths missed the first time around. This is a personal path designed to be walked prayerfully in the company of your inner support team.

Exercises: The Path through Grief

In addition to sharing with you my journey through grief, and the gifts and insight I gained along the way, I'm going to show you some meditation exercises to practice. Even if you've never meditated before, it's OK; I will walk you through the process. Meditation is just another word for awareness of breathing, and it is one of the most precious gifts I received through my wounding. Every morning, I meditate and bring my son's spirit into my space.

Set aside between ten and fifteen minutes to complete each of the exercises provided throughout the book. They will help you put into practice what I'm sharing with you here. Many of the exercises are meant to be repeated on a regular basis until they replace the old grooves in the brain. Reading something once is not enough to retrain our habits that may have been established for years. However, repeated use of these tools will create change that you will see quickly, usually within a few weeks of regular use. Deepak Chopra says it takes twenty-one days to establish a habit; that's not very long when you have the tools. Using the MP3 guided meditations will yield the strongest results, as they add an auditory tool to deepen the new learning. Together, we'll embark on the process of weaving a new way of life from the pieces of the old.

Guided Meditations

I am with you as you go, not only in spirit but through my website, *www.theresetappouni.com,* where you can contact me with questions or concerns. I encourage you to download the MP3 of most of the guided work on the site. The MP3 features my voice over the beautiful compositions of Grammy-nominated composer Michael Hoppé and "Heart and Soul Meditations" produced by Lance Ware. It's time to begin. Your journey is waiting.

Journaling

I recommend that you keep a journal as you read this book to help you navigate your path through grief and chart your progress. For one thing, it is a record of your journey that you will treasure later. Second, your journal is a place to release and confide all your feelings, and it will bring you more clarity than reading my words alone possibly can. Write in your journal on a regular basis so that you remain aware of your desired outcomes.

As William Shakespeare wrote:

Give sorrow words: the grief that does not speak
Whispers the o'er-fraught heart and bids it break.

—Macbeth

Choice

Loss is like a mudslide that plummets down a mountain and into the middle of our river of life. The old channel is now blocked and we are being forced into the new. We will never be the same again. That's why I say grief never ends. It changes us for life—it actually changes us into a different way of living. But we have a choice in how we will be changed. Will we choose to live out our days in darkness, frozen solid, or will we search for the meaning and gifts surrounding loss?

> **Grief never ends. It changes us for life—it actually changes us into a different way of living. But we have a choice in how we will be changed.**

Throughout this book, you will be taking steps that will lead you to your best life. What we are doing with each thought and action in our lives is choosing. There is a quote from A Course in Miracles that helps me with this a lot:

Every decision I make is a choice between a grievance and a miracle.

I relinquish all regrets, grievances and resentments and I choose the miracle.

Daily, as I find myself approaching events or people with regret or resentment, I say this to myself and ask to be shown a different perspective. Each time we make a decision, we have moved through choices into choice. Our awareness is the only difference between what happens in our life by conscious choosing and what happens *to* us without our input—also known as unconscious choice. We can choose our intention using the skills we'll learn along the journey of grief.

Each Person Grieves Differently

In twentieth-century psychology and psychiatry, it was widely accepted in the medical world that a patient should get through the initial stages of acute grief in a couple of months. We find that ridiculous now, but at the time medicine drew a circle around pain and loss, and patients were expected to move on, leaving that circle behind like an excised tumor. The truth is that grief is a journey requiring as much time as the individual needs. Ancient cultures knew and honored the long dark night of the heart and soul known as grief, but as we entered the self-focused mechanical years following the industrial revolution, we began to build a belief system based on the logic of the brain. We put the heart aside.

The eminent Dr. Elisabeth Kübler-Ross changed how we approached death with her theory of the five stages of grief: denial, anger, bargaining, depression, and acceptance. Her insights were often misapplied, using our modern focus on the brain to set this up as a standard one-size-fits-all process. Even if you *do* go through all of these steps along the way, you may not necessarily follow them in the order listed or remain in each stage for equal amounts of time. You will recycle through the stages as time goes on. There is comfort in being able to say, "Ah, I'm going through that step," but to me there is a danger in wondering whether we have missed a key stage or are progressing too quickly or too slowly through the stages. We may follow them in order, in reverse order, or, most often, at random, and perhaps even experience a stage that's not even listed. Human emotions are rarely predictable, as they are not symptoms of disease but an individual's way of coping with loss.

Now we find modern medicine once again deciding that we can all fit in one box. According to the June 2011 issue of *Scientific American*, there are proposed changes to the fifth edition of *Diagnostic and Statistical Manual of Mental Disorders* (DSM) due in 2013. This is the bible of the mental health community. Because grieving and clinical depression have similar symptoms, the current DSM prohibits prescribing psychiatric medications until two months after the death of a loved one, which is already a questionable proposition. Two months to grieve, and then if we aren't "over it," we're given a prescription that labels us in need of medication that may have multiple side effects and whose purpose is to cover up our grieving? How do we assume that everyone will complete the grieving process in that time frame? If they haven't, is the best route to mask the feelings with pharmaceuticals? Shutting down the emotional body makes it much more difficult to tune in to our feelings and move through grief in a heart-centered way. In the proposal for 2013, this time frame is reduced from two months to two weeks. Can it be true that the people who wrote this new rule never suffered a loss? Or have they bought into the material values of a society who only sees our productivity in the world and excises anything that interferes? What is the fear if we experience our emotions and work through them in the heart? We are human; we are supposed to *feel*.

Dr. Allen Frances, the Duke University School of Medicine psychiatrist who served as lead author of the current rules, calls the changes "a disaster." Symptoms like sadness and loss of appetite "are completely typical of normal grieving, but DSM-5 would instead label you with a mental disorder."

We live in a culture that has no patience for sadness or dealing with loss, and this new development shines a spotlight on that truth. Cold, hard rules encourage us who are grieving to just move on and not burden others with our emotions. I know one thing from my own experience of grief, and from the experiences of clients and participants in my workshops who are finding their way: the time frame is as individual as fingerprints.

If you get nothing else from this book, please know that your journey is your own—and don't let anyone tell you otherwise.

If you get nothing else from this book, please know that your journey is your own—and don't let anyone tell you otherwise. Of course medicine helps those who feel so deeply depressed that they consider harmful behaviors, including suicide. But the process of grieving takes as long as it takes. Please be patient. To deny the pain is to simply put it off until later. Holding the pain in the body eventually causes other symptoms, so it is in our best interests physically to move into healing. My goal is to help you move through the pain and into the larger life that grief is carving out in you.

From this point on, please don't allow yourself to enter into the comparison game with others about their loss and pain being greater or less than your own. It's disconcerting to hear someone say their experience is worse than yours; but there are others who ask how they can be suffering when someone else's loss seems so much worse. The cells of our body can't quantitatively measure the amount of grief you or I feel; there's no computer program capable of registering and then ranking your feelings and emotions versus mine. All of these are useless comparisons. So don't compare yourself to anyone. All your body knows is that you are sad, lonely, depressed, hurting. Comfort others when you can, but for the moment focus on helping yourself.

It is a heroic quest, and one I will take with you, supporting and encouraging your personal journey. I honor your courage in opening this book. I applaud your courage in exposing your wound for healing. Part of this book will be a sharing of the journey that was my grief, though I know everyone's path is different. However, since no one gets a pass on grief, it's good to know you are not alone. Come, let's begin.

The Hero's Journey

To open deeply, as genuine spiritual life requires, we need tremendous courage and strength, a kind of warrior spirit. But the place for this warrior strength is in the heart.

—Jack Kornfield, *A Path with Heart*

Though real human experiences are invaluable to us, we often rely on books and movies to show us how heroes and heroines overcome difficult problems. Our mainstream media, through storylines and actors, is supplying us with the modern version of epic myths. Stories are modeled from ancient journeys and share the bravery of those who came before us, but, more importantly, they give the viewer a glimpse of hope. The road through grief is a heroic journey. The Indiana Jones movies are a modern example, as are the Lord of the Rings trilogy, *Star Wars,* and many others. But tales like these have been recorded for more than five thousand years.

From the *Epic of Gilgamesh, Inanna's Descent to the Underworld, Beowulf,* and the *Iliad,* to modern films and books like *The Fisher King, The Wizard of Oz,* and the Harry Potter series, writers and filmmakers have used the hero's journey as a vehicle for telling the story of our mythic adventures moving from our potential self to our enlightened, beautiful self through hostile territory and grievous suffering. The journey mirrors our grief; that's why I've modeled this book after the hero/heroine's journey. Some of you may be familiar with Joseph Campbell's *The Hero with a Thousand Faces,* where we first learn about the "hero's journey," but the journey through grief is different in substantive ways. The following is the pivotal scene from *Indiana Jones and the Last Crusade.*

*There's Indy, leaning out over the edge of a deep chasm
full of sharp boulders. The holy grail is a hundred feet
away on the other side, with no way across. So close,
but unattainable. Behind him, his father lies mortally
wounded, and he knows only the grail can save him.
Still, he is mangled, exhausted, clinging to what appears
to be his last foothold and out of options. He hears his
father call out that he should take a leap of faith into
the void. Fear and grief are clear on Indy's face and in
his body, but what choice does he have? Great evil, and
his wounded father, are behind him—his only hope lies
ahead. He leaps, claws at the opposite cliff for a moment,
and falls. What happens next stuns everyone—he lands
on a brilliantly camouflaged bridge placed there by the
knights who guard the grail.*

Indy's faith that there is more out there than he can possibly
understand saves him. But first, he had to be in a place of darkness where nothing else worked. He had to rely on an unfamil-
iar belief that there was something more than he understood in
his education as a scientist and a modern man. He had to accept
that his brain was not going to help him. He had to rely on his
heart's strength. He had to hear the call.

Unfortunately, for those of us who are suffering, our journey
doesn't happen in a ninety-minute time frame. If we are griev-

ing the death of a loved one, we will grieve for our entire lifetime. That is a fact. Thankfully, it's in our power to transform
our grief as we travel to find the grail, or the gift, in our journey.

The Many Faces of Grief

So much of our grief is stored from events that we have ignored
or buried as they were happening, and for a big portion of this
book we'll look deeply at past grieving you might be holding
with you today without even realizing it.

The following list is meant to help you ferret out all the ways
grief has touched you. Some will be pretty obvious, others less
so. Read through the list, and record in your journal all of the
circumstances that have been present in your life. Please take
your time; no event is too small to matter.

Individual Grief

To start, let's examine some of the more obvious ways you may
have experienced grief.

+ Death of a parent(s)
+ Death of a child (including miscarriage, stillborn child,
  abortion)
+ Death of a sibling
+ Death of a spouse
+ Death or loss of a close friend

- Death of a pet
- Alcohol- or drug-addicted parent(s)
- Divorce (your own or your parents')
- Safety issues, such as bullying or abuse
- Loss of your religious faith
- Moving when a child
- Moving and leaving your friends and/or community for a job
- Loss of a job
- Financial disaster, such as a loss of home or business
- Birth of a child with health problems or disabilities
- Involvement in war (as a combatant or civilian)
- Loss of someone close to you due to Alzheimer's or dementia
- Long-term or chronic illness (yourself or others)
- Aging losses—health, beauty, etc.
- And anything else that you know that you grieve for

Global Grief

Our world gives us many reasons to feel sadness and grief. Global grief is a bit harder to pin down than individual losses, but it is very real nonetheless. It occurs outside our private lives and affects us as a community. As I complete this book, thousands across the Northeast are suffering loss from Hurricane Sandy. Not only are individuals, homes, pets, neighbors, and years of memories gone, but a really deep fear over the future of our planet has come to the surface. Though everyone involved, and those who are connected in other ways, will never return to their lives as they were, something else is happening. The gifts that are arising in this tragedy are many—neighbors are helping neighbors, and awareness of our fragile ecosystem is surfacing. The gifts are small, but they have mighty results, and they will weave themselves into the grieving process.

Joanna Macy, eco-philosopher, scholar in the fields of systems theory and deep ecology, and a voice for peace throughout the world, says about global grief:

We are in grief. With all that's being inflicted on the natural world and the social fabric of our lives together, there's fear too, anger as well. These responses are natural and healthy. If we disown them, we cripple our vitality and intelligence.

So we bow to them instead. When pain for the world arises within you, recognize it and pause. Pause and breathe, as if making room for it . . . Realize that you are capable of suffering with your world.

Sometimes we can take solace in shared experiences—we just need to recognize that there are outside factors contributing to our grief.

- ✦ Energetic (feeling sad or crying, with no specific explanation why)

- ✦ War anywhere

- ✦ Catastrophe

- ✦ Natural disaster, such as an earthquake, hurricane, or tsunami

- ✦ Events particular to the United States (e.g., the assassination of John F. Kennedy, Martin Luther King, Jr., and Robert F. Kennedy; the Space Shuttle *Challenger* disaster; 9/11)

- ✦ Global fears (e.g., child slavery, unstable governments and citizen unrest, hunger, climate change)

- ✦ And anything else that you grieve for

Are you surprised by the number of losses you have experienced in your lifetime? Or by how few you've endured? As you read on, other things may come up; add them to your original list. We sometimes have enormous reservoirs of grief that are latent until we experience a loss that triggers the old pains. The list is simply to alert you that you have many things that are considered losses in your life, even if you yourself have glossed over them and stored them away. Your emotional body, the part of you that feels, knows where they are, and the heart finds them when you are open. Grief is one of the greatest heart-openers and healers of all time.

The wounds we suffer are all deaths of some kind. They may be small or large, but they are deaths nonetheless. Not getting into a school we desired, losing a job, suffering an illness, getting a divorce, moving, breaking up, seeing children all over the world abused and starved—all of these are causes for grieving. They all represent what we see as lost possibilities. The possibilities of the job, the home, the things, the relationship, the promise of children and what they represent to us and to the outside world—these are what we mourn. Some of the things we lost involved many years of envisioning, working, and praying. The truth is that they are not lost but need to be revisited and revised.

Grief is one of the greatest heart-openers and healers of all time.

Remember, you're a different person now. The body, including the heart, doesn't sort losses out into categories—it feels our sadness, our fear, and our questioning of ourselves, and it begins the process of grief.

Before Reading *The Gifts of Grief*

On a scale of 1–10, with 10 being the strongest and 1 being the weakest, rank how strong each of the following emotions is. Breathe deeply, go to your heart for the true answers, and circle the number. You will do this exercise again at the end of the book—this is to give you an idea of where you're at to start.

	Emotions/Body					Rank						
1	Sadness	1	2	3	4	5	6	7	8	9	10
2	Anger	1	2	3	4	5	6	7	8	9	10
3	Resentment	1	2	3	4	5	6	7	8	9	10
4	Lack of energy	1	2	3	4	5	6	7	8	9	10
5	Loss of interest in life	1	2	3	4	5	6	7	8	9	10
6	Gratitude	1	2	3	4	5	6	7	8	9	10
7	Hope	1	2	3	4	5	6	7	8	9	10
8	Breathing skills	1	2	3	4	5	6	7	8	9	10

First Step: Just Be for a While

So, what do we do? First, we must learn, or relearn, being. Just be for a while; allow your heart to hurt, allow your brain to ask "why?" and allow your body to rest. Grief, loss, and anger take a huge toll. Without time for rest, the stress on the body can turn into illness. This cocooning period takes as long as it takes—you cannot rush it. It depends on how willing you are to release the pain. Only after time has passed can you begin the long process of exploring your grief, healing your wounds, and asking the important question: "Where is the light in the darkness of this loss?"

Shifting Your Perspective

Many of us have encountered the poem and treatise "The Dark Night of the Soul" by Saint John of the Cross, which is about the suffering revealed along the path to oneness with God. In modern day usage, the dark night refers to those times when we are lost in illness, grief, doubt, or confusion. Mother Teresa revealed her long struggle with her doubts about her faith and works, referring to it as her dark night of the soul.

Matthew Fox also speaks of a similar darkness and courage:

Facing the darkness, admitting the pain, allowing the pain to be pain, is never easy. This is why courage—big heartedness—is the most essential virtue on the spiritual journey. But if we fail to let pain be pain—and our entire patriarchal culture refuses to let this happen—then pain will haunt us in nightmarish ways. We will become pain's victims instead of the healers we might become.

—Original Blessing

If you accept that you are now in that place of darkness, it is time to decide if you are willing to explore and bring in the light. Your heart has been bruised and battered, and yet here I am asking you to expose its very core. I promise you, your heart is the center of your strength. This is not the time to put up walls or listen to those who are uncomfortable with your grief.

> **I promise you, your heart is the center of your strength. This is not the time to put up walls.**

You probably picked up this book because you or someone you care about are currently in a place of loss. Something has occurred that demands you acknowledge change, whether you like it or not. You are being asked to take a new path. Going deeply into grief is to leave a familiar place and landscape behind and encounter the "dark night of the soul." Sacred and secular writers have been using this reference for centuries, seeing it as the perfect definition for where we are in the deepest and most hopeless times of our grief and despair. But don't be afraid; with your willingness, a guide/helper will appear to see you through.

Your First Ally—Your Heart

Your dark night of the soul isn't strong enough to withstand the light of the heart. Living your extraordinary, beautiful life is only possible through a new view of what it means to be human. Great courage is required to effect powerful changes. You are being asked to step through the door of fear into a totally new room of belief in order to access the gifts in your grieving. That sound you are hearing from the depths of your heart is the *cri de coeur*—the cry from the heart. It's time to call upon all the support you have available to you in this journey so far—your faith, your guidance, your intuitive self, and, above all, the whole you that was created to experience this life.

The fact that you are reading this book tells me that you have courage and have heard the cry of your heart, and I am grateful for that. I ask you to commit to trying one small thing right now—meditation. I hope you have the MP3 downloads of guided visualizations, but if not, read through this a few times and then guide yourself. You can also record the words in your own voice.

Meditation

Meditation, as I teach it, is the simple act of going into the moment and allowing ourselves to just be. Each time something comes into our minds, we let it go like clouds in the sky and return to the present moment. Eventually we will begin to stay there for longer periods of time and achieve an element of peace. All is takes is a mastery of the art of breathing. Inhale slowly; exhale slowly. Let the thoughts drift; tell them you'll get to them later. Inhale; exhale. Throughout the day, again, we need to check our breathing frequently. When we ask throughout the day: "Where is my breath? How deep is it?" we open the possibility of peace, if only for a moment. These moments will grow and build as the question becomes a habit.

The great teacher Alan Watts reminds us how to be in the moment:

We could say that meditation doesn't have a reason or doesn't have a purpose. In this respect it's unlike almost all other things we do except perhaps making music and dancing. When we make music we don't do it in order to reach a certain point, such as the end of the composition. If that were the purpose of music then obviously the fastest players would be the best. Also, when we are dancing we are not aiming to arrive at a particular place on the floor as in taking a journey. When we dance, the journey itself is the point, as when we play music the playing itself is the point. And exactly the same thing is true in meditation. Meditation is the discovery that the point of life is always arrived at in the immediate moment.

—The Essence of Alan Watts

With that in mind, let's begin with our first exercise.

Grief Work: Exercise 1

Healing Your Heart, Part I

We'll start with a basic visualization to help open your heart. Practice this every day and whenever the uncomfortable whys and what-ifs and fearful or angry thoughts batter your body.

1. Sit quietly in a chair with your feet flat on the floor, or lie down if you feel the need. Close your eyes. Breathe in deeply. Breathe out.

2. On the exhale, allow thoughts to float out of your head like moths set free. Watch them go, fluttering their soft wings, glad to be released. Breathe.

3. Inhale again, deeply. Let your shoulders soften and your chest relax. Take your time. When you feel your shoulders drop, even slightly, go to the next step. Breathe.

4. Now move the inhalation of breath to the area of your heart. Sense your heart, wounded and struggling. Its pain may even prevent you from taking a full, healing breath, but gently, gently continue to try. Just breathe, as deeply as you can.

5. As you inhale, see your body surrounded with vibrating golden light. Breathe in the golden light, filling your chest, bathing your grieving heart. Breathe.

6. Inhale the light, and exhale the darkness, slowly replacing grief and fear with love. Feel your heart settle into a steady beat. Just allow the slow breathing, the sensation

of light, and your steady heart to fill your body with feelings of peace and calm. Breathe in this peace and calm, from your head to your toes.

7. Continue to sit and breathe for a few minutes, or as long as you feel comfortable. When you're ready, open your eyes.

Breathing into the heart will release the true, intuitive message of your guidance, not the self-constructed or societal downloads of the brain. Until we trust in our hearts, there will be no progress, and no understanding of the process of grief.

Until we trust in our hearts, there will be no progress, and no understanding of the process of grief.

Avoiding Busy

Between grief and nothing, I will take grief.

—William Faulkner

Why should we choose grief over nothing? Aren't there times when feeling nothing would be a relief? The truth is, it's the pain that makes us fully human. With all of the busyness in our lives, many people who are grieving get even busier so they can ignore the pain. This coping mechanism is one that our culture accepts. Our friends and loved ones can deal with *busy*. At least we're doing something they understand. I've worked with many clients who turned to alcohol, drugs, or excessive increases in time spent working, watching television, or exercising.

To stop and make room to hear the heart makes most people anxious. Except for those who sink into depression, being still is seen by the grieving as a place to remember things they don't want to remember, to dwell on sadness. Perceived busyness is one of the reasons friends and family might find it hard to talk to us about our problems. If we seem busy, or focused elsewhere, they feel they will be bringing something up that we're managing to ignore for the time being. And sometimes they're right. On the other hand, many people who are grieving a death say that friends and family act like the person never existed. This is more painful for them than talking about their loved one, which they see as a way to keep their memory alive.

We need to learn to tell our friends and family what we need so they won't have to make assumptions. One day, I got still. I was used to meditating at that point and open to the possibility that my heart would speak to me. In that stillness I asked my heart to tell me what it wanted. I asked it to tell me its story. And in response I heard an inner voice that is with me to this day. I was able to hear and was blessed with the knowing of my heart's whisper.

This conundrum of wanting to heal but knowing the only way is *through* the pain is all the more reason we should go to the heart. To do that, we need to get brave, and get quiet in the mind. It's time to bring in peace and calm.

Grief Work: Exercise 2

Listening to Your Heart, Part I

Perform this exercise at the end of your day, just before bed. If you like, you may play some soft, meditative music with this work. Many grieving people are not ready to hear music in their space, and that's fine. When you can, incorporate music that helps you to relax. I recommend some wonderful music in the appendix.

1. Sit quietly in a chair with your feet flat on the floor, or lie down if you feel the need. Close your eyes. Breathe into your heart for a count of five and then exhale through your heart for a count of five.

2. As you breathe, connect once again with your heart. Think of something that makes you feel peaceful, and breathe that into your chest. It could be a place you love to sit and watch the sunset; the feel of a child's face resting near your neck; the up-and-down tummy of a sleeping puppy. Choose something very simple. Concentrate on recalling the emotions that you feel in this particular time and place. Feel the calm and peace throughout your body.

3. Once you have that feeling of peace in your body, breathe it into your heart.

4. When you are relaxed and focused on your heart, ask your heart this question: *Heart, tell me, please. What are you feeling?* Sit peacefully and quietly and wait for an answer.

5. You may not be ready to know the answer on this particular evening, but wait quietly and see. You will, at some point, hear a quiet whisper from your heart's space with the answer to your question.

When you are ready, open your eyes and write in your journal about this experience. It will help you next time you want to repeat the exercise. When you are ready to go to bed, ask to hear your heart's message in your dreams. Keep your journal by your bed so you can write anything you remember as soon as you awaken. We forget dreams so quickly, and they are often important messages from our higher self.

Now that you are in touch with your heart, you have your most important ally on your journey. If you think about some of your favorite stories, movies, or books, you will probably notice that the hero or heroine always has one or more allies, or helpers, on their journey. Dorothy from *The Wizard of Oz* had her loyal dog, Toto; *The Lord of the Rings'* Frodo Baggins had Samwise Gamgee. Both companions, who accompany our heroes from the start, represent the same first and greatest ally that we all have available to us—our hearts. In this journey, your heart is your number one companion, friend, and ally. As we move forward, other allies will show themselves.

It's time to ask yourself, gently, if you have the courage—the heart—to begin the journey to healing. The next two exercises were created to help you choose with strength. Begin with Exercise 3, repeating it every day for about a week. After a week of practice, then add Exercise 4.

Note: You are laying the groundwork for receiving the gifts of your heart here—this is important preparation for your journey. You will not be asked to do as many exercises in the following chapters.

Grief Work: Exercise 3

Healing Your Heart, Part II

Now that you have tried the practice of breathing described earlier, I ask you to add a step. The beginning of this work will be familiar. Use the MP3 or read through this several times, then close your eyes and do the exercise.

1. Sit quietly in a chair with your feet flat on the floor, or lie down if you feel the need. Close your eyes. Breathe in deeply. Breathe out.

2. On the exhale, allow thoughts to float out of your head like moths set free. Watch them go, fluttering their soft wings, glad to be released. Breathe.

3. Inhale again, deeply, deeply, letting your shoulders soften and your chest relax. Breathe.

4. Now move the inhalation to the area of your heart. Sense your heart, wounded and struggling. Its pain may even prevent you from taking a full, healing breath, but gently continue to try.

5. As you inhale, see your body surrounded with vibrating golden light. Breathe in the golden light, filling your chest, bathing your grieving heart.

6. Inhale the light, and exhale the darkness, slowly visualizing fear and grief leaving and love arriving. Feel your heart settle into a steady beat. Breathe.

7. Allow the slow breathing, the sensation of light, and your steady heart to fill your body with feelings of peace and calm. Breathe in peace and calm, from your head to your toes.

8. After you have relaxed, and your heart is beating rhythmically and slowly, picture your heart. Ask your heart to show itself to you as it is emotionally. In other words, what it would look like if it showed on its surface all the pain, scars, disappointments, and grief. Take your time, breathe deeply, and allow your heart to show itself to you. Breathe.

9. When you have a picture in your mind, tell your heart that you want to help it heal. Tell your heart that you want it to be healthy, robust, and vibrant, and you are

grateful for all that it does for you. Do this in your own words, breathing deeply.

10. Now, see your wounded heart bathed once again in light, but this time it is a warm pink light. Then visualize the bumps, bruises, cuts, gouges, and broken pieces coming together and healing in this beautiful pink light. Continue to breathe deeply in this place until you are ready to open your eyes.

Take some time to just sit quietly, breathe, and notice any changes in how you feel, physically and emotionally. This would be a good time to write in your journal so you can follow your progress. One visualization won't be enough, but doing this over and over will result in beautiful healing.

Grief Work: Exercise 4

Listening to Your Heart, Part II

Once you've practiced Exercises 1–3 a few times and feel successful with them, you're ready for Exercise 4.

1. Prepare in the same way as Exercise 3, but this time, ask a different question of your heart: *Heart, tell me, please. What is it I can do to help heal you?*

2. Wait quietly, listening for the inner whisper that will share information that is very important for you to know. From day to day, it may take varying amounts of time for you

to become calm and focus on your heart. Be at peace as much as possible.

As always, please note anything in your journal that you want to remember. Even noting your attempt will help to focus you on the path.

The work you are being asked to do here is the purpose and meaning of the heart. It's important that you notice and have feelings about your heart, since your heart is the first ally on your journey. Think of this as voluntarily putting aside whatever old creaky armor keeps you from hearing your heart. You will be grateful that you decided to listen to its wisdom.

We have only begun this journey together, but I hope that you have seen the value of the tools you have within you. Your breath, your heart and your inner guidance are all accessible without fancy, expensive purchases. You have been given the possibility of healing within your own body, soul, and mind. Just being conscious of your breathing can change the way you live your life. All of these are gifts from your incredibly complex, yet wonderfully simple, self.

Chapter 2

Overcoming Fear
and Judgment

Hidden in every event of your life is a possible epiphany about
love. God's love is beyond death.

—Deepak Chopra, *The Path to Love*

There is no healing without courage. Be brave! The journey
to finding your gifts will lead to challenges and struggles.
Going inside, meeting your darkness, and confronting your own
fear and grief, stripped of your usual strengths and defenses, is
part of the process of growth and grieving.

Loss is a wound that creates a sea change in the way we see
and experience our lives. It can't be healed in our emotional body
by applying a poultice of science, religion, or any other measure-
ment. Grief is as individual as our face or our fingerprints. It

changes in its course, weaving itself into our life fabric in thin silken threads and thick woolen tangles. It appears as a darker bordering, a contrast that reveals the depth and vibrancy of life's daily experience. For most of us, the epiphany of love is hidden, waiting to be discovered.

In 1998, shortly after I met my partner Lance, I was blessed to have the words of my son come through when Lance and I were in a church meditating on the Universal Day of Peace. This experience lifted me to another level of healing in my grief and was only possible because my heart was open. It was the first time I'd had a visual and physical image of Michael's energy, and we both felt it at the same time.

Later, in 2005, I had another epiphany. I had been suffering for some time with a chronic and painful condition. No facet of modern medicine was helping. At the time, I was studying with the amazing teacher, philosopher, and writer Jean Houston, and I was becoming more aware of my need to connect to my higher self and my spiritual guidance in order to heal.

Jean was having a weeklong retreat focused on healing at a Catholic center in the Chicago area, and Lance and I decided to go. The weekend was filled with ritual and focus on the healing processes used from the beginning of written time, and probably before. We were part of a healing group similar to the ones Asclepius, the father of medicine, created around the year 300 BCE. It was in this sacred atmosphere that I found myself participating in a ritual in the beautiful church on the campus.

As we walked slowly in procession by candlelight, I paused near a statue of the Blessed Mother. Words cannot describe the sense of peace and sacredness that filled my body. I felt my heart weep tears of joy. And then I felt the impression of hands on my shoulders, a pressure that was pure energy. I knew that presence immediately and was wrapped in the essence of Michael. I felt a ripple of energy throughout my body and then a complete feeling of being embraced and at home again. In my heart I heard his voice and the words that he spoke before his energy disappeared and I was once more aware of the church. What he said, and what I will always remember, is: "Your wound is not a wound but a portal."

A Gift

Your grief has opened a portal, a place where you can access more than healing.

Those words changed my way of grieving and were the inspiration for my writing this book. As I understand it, without the grievous wound I had suffered, I would not have experienced a way forward into my highest self and my soul's purpose. If we can each accept that we are on this planet to create a life desired by our soul, we can become exactly who we are meant to be. Our sufferings are not tests of our faith. Our sufferings can take down our defenses and allow us to open to all experiences, including those of the sacred. To do this, we cannot stay focused on our suffering. We must enter the portal provided by our wound where we will find the answers and the healing we never dreamed possible. Giving up our doubts and meditating are the keys to the portal.

Meanwhile, we have to contend with how the world is and how it will react to our suffering. It's not easy to resume our place in daily life when we have been visited by grief and then by messengers and messages from a place we do not know. It requires that we become aware of the three worlds we live in—that of the soul, the heart, and the mind. In the worlds of the soul and the heart, there is no longer any place for hate, judgment, or guilt. The soul is the essence of who we are, and no one has ever pinpointed where that essence is located. We are aware of the direction given by the soul, and its work is done through the heart, the emotional/intuitive brain of our body. The mind is a place of logic and rarely helps in the realm of emotions, such as grief. We can't make this geographic and sacred leap without intention and being aware of our challenges.

Grief Leaves Us Powerless

Perhaps the deepest wounding in grief is our realization that we are not in control and we are not safe. We've spent a lifetime preparing for every possibility, protecting ourselves and our loved ones by buying safe cars, making sure we wear seatbelts, stopping smoking, getting regular medical check-ups, submitting to vaccinations, living in secure neighborhoods, taking herbs and vitamins, and doing crossword puzzles to avoid Alzheimer's. The list is exhausting. Lately even grocery stores provide hand sanitizer to kill germs on our shopping carts. Despite all of our precautions, warning systems, and protections put in place, this *thing* still got through.

We were good people following all the rules, living as we were directed, and our sense of betrayal is hard to focus. Where does this judgment belong? On our parents for telling us everything would be all right? On our schools? What about the church? What about society itself for promising us rewards for good behavior? Or is it our own fault for being so innocent we believed we were safe?

Our world thrives on dichotomy: it's us versus them. The good will win and the bad will lose, whether it's a football game or a war. The atmosphere of sports thrives on each side's fans defining the other as somehow "unworthy." This small competition carries over into the worlds of business and politics, and, finally, into defining people all over the globe according to their religion or skin color. Inside us, without our knowledge, the knowing grows that we are the ones who are safe. We are not *them*.

That brings up the big unmentionable. Why not just blame God?

Losing Faith

Research shows that people with a lifetime commitment to a spiritual belief or practice will often move to an acceptance based on their beliefs. Then there are those, like me, who reject their faith, move away from it, and finally find the way back to a different view. How can we compare those two ways? They are equally valid and must be honored. If we were raised in a religion that presents God as the creator of everything, always in charge, it seems fair to question why this pain has been sent to us.

My reaction to the loss of my son was deeply connected to my religious childhood. From the time I was five years old, I knelt every night beside my bed to pray before I lay down. My guardian angel was real and comforting. From my childhood twin bed, to my college dorm bed (where I endured a lot of teasing), to the bed I shared with my husband, I still knelt at night and said the same prayers of gratitude I'd said as a child, plus a few pertinent supplications based on the day's events. Through my father's alcoholism and my loss of friends, pets, and homes, I spent a lot of time on my knees. When Michael lay in the ICU, my need was huge, and it touched into all the early sadness I hadn't acknowledged. Again, I went to my knees. The small chapel in the hospital was my place of refuge. By the time Michael died, my knees were bruised from the days and nights of supplication.

The day he died, my husband and I drove home from the hospital in silence. That night I went upstairs and climbed directly into my side of the king-sized bed, lying rigid until morning, refusing the solace of my lifelong connection with God, the Blessed Mother, and my special angels. Oblivious, I had added another grief to the list—my loss of belief and comfort. I had lived an honest and prayerful life, followed the rules, and what had happened? Despite my pleas and my promises of more service, the worst of all possible things had happened—my child had died before me. In all those years of orthodox behavior, I never once saw my kneeling in prayer as an attempt to control my surroundings and protect me and mine from something unnamed and too frightening to acknowledge. Yet it was as much a part of my effort to outwit life's possibilities as the greens and vitamins I served my children.

I was mad at God, and I felt betrayed. Even though I had no anger toward the woman who hit Michael, I had anger toward God that threatened to explode in me. I rejected all the rituals I believed should have protected me. Strangely, I never included Jesus in this anger, and chose "Suffer the Little Children to Come to Me" for Michael's gravestone. My rational mind saw how Jesus, Mary, and my son had all suffered. Only God had not. I continued to go to church, but all I did there was cry. I found no solace, no comfort, and no reassurance. I was betrayed, and as long as I believed God had a hand in this, a direct hand, I was no longer his loving child.

I read recently about a minister who said he would be surprised if someone who lost a child or a partner unexpectedly didn't have a lapse of faith and question God. He is a wise soul. Those of us who challenge our beliefs usually search deeply into their meaning and create a much stronger and deeper spiritual life. It's not a matter of clinging to dogma but actually choosing to find the presence of what we think of as God in our soul.

Frequently, as I did, we will throw out the whole idea of God. We can't find him in such darkness. But once we have done the work of forgiveness, we will recover the presence of God. I recovered the rituals and beauty of the goddess of the church, the Blessed Mother, and recreated them in my home in the form of flower-filled altars and objects of spiritual devotion.

There was a point when, if you would have asked me, I wouldn't have believed that I would come to a place in my spiritual journey when all of that Father/daughter angst between God and me would mean nothing. But when we redefine God as love, not as a patriarchal Father in charge of every moment in our lives, we change forever. When we see the universe as a loving place no matter what happens, we refocus on our own responsibility for how we handle our life challenges. This was a gift, received after a long process which I describe in this book. I had to turn to my heart, forgive, and release before blame became part of the me that began the journey.

A Gift

Moving from blame to loving acceptance is one of the most amazing results of following the path of love.

Another Kind of Betrayal

I saw my divorce from my husband after thirty-six years of marriage as another betrayal. I had followed the plan, created a nurturing home, raised our children, and squeezed my dream of writing into a small corner of my world. Oh, my list of grievances was long! I had created a place of safety, once again, and even with the example of Michael's death I expected the magic protection to hold. I hadn't learned, yet. It was a long time before I could look back and recognize my own contributions to the disintegration of what had outlasted itself. My husband courageously faced the fact that our relationship was over. It doesn't matter *how* he mirrored that to me, but that he did. I received a gift so I could move forward. When one partner in a marriage changes, the other partner has a couple of ways they can go. We can ask questions, try to be understanding, and try to be supportive, or we can stand our ground and say "I want the person I married back."

The changes delivered to me through grief and loss caused me to become a different person spiritually and emotionally. By denying who I had become and wishing I would go back to who I had been, my husband forced me to make a choice. I could stay married and bury my true self forever, or I could face the grief of separation and loss of the life we had built together and find my freedom. His anger and disappointment led me to the path of freedom. There are those who will support who you are, and their gifts are easy to see. Those people or institutions who oppose our growth and our path are every bit as successful in showing us the way, if we don't surrender.

A Gift

Frequently, another person will act in a way we find painful, upsetting, or grievous. It may be years before we can see them as a giver of a gift.

⌒

My journey, like most, would move forward, double back on itself, repeat steps, and eventually become comfortable, but first I had to drop my belief in the idea of safety and control. I also needed to strengthen my heart awareness of millions of others who were in the midst of their own life changing through accident, illness, war, and crime until it became an essential part of my healing. Once I did those things, I would recover my faith in God.

When we are in the early stages of grief, none of this is in our hearts. Only pain resides there. When we express a crisis of faith, like I did, others who still reside in the surety of their faith or their denial become very alarmed. Some will pray for us, certain that we have faltered and therefore are suffering greatly. Still locked in a sense of safety and control, they don't want to ever be where we are. Seeing us angry, sad, and grieving is difficult, and they will call upon their tools to help us. And often we will refuse. If you do, you may lose friends for good, as your refusal arouses their fear. This loss will temporarily become part of the grief process. Soon we will understand that only those who love us for who we really are can truly be a part of our soul's life.

Open Your Heart

When we open our hearts just a crack, even begrudgingly, and decide to let a little light in, we create the moment when each one of us will choose to step out of bitterness or depression just enough to say yes to our own heroic journey. At first we may refuse, but when we do, our first ally—the heart—will come forward to give us the courage to move onto the dimly lit path of change. We must continue to be open to allow for other allies, friends, and compatriots to assist and guide us. The process of conscious meditation is invaluable if this is to happen.

Conscious Breathing

But how do we prepare to be open? The first step I've shared is being conscious of our breathing. It sounds so simple, yet the breath is the vehicle that takes us to healing. Start to notice how you breathe throughout the day. When we were children we used to breathe with a natural rhythm, inhaling deeply through the abdomen, creating energy in our beings. As we get older, our stresses and fears begin to control our breathing, and we start to breathe shallowly, high in the chest. If you can picture a baby or a puppy at rest, their stomachs rise and fall in an even, beautiful rhythm. This breath brings everything into the body that is needed for attention and energy. The shallow breaths we produce now as adults, particularly when we're under stress, can't release the toxins that are building in our bodies, let alone bring in the healthy effects of oxygen.

For now, all I ask you to do is to be aware at random moments throughout your day of how you are breathing. Every once in a while, just stop and notice the breath. Notice *where* you are breathing. Is your breath high in your chest? Are your shoulders tight and restricting your space? Are you breathing short, shallow breaths, and sometimes sighing deeply? Or are you inhaling slowly and peacefully, filling your lungs from top to bottom, then exhaling fully, releasing the breath with a brief pause before you take the next inhale? Don't try to control your breath; simply allow your body to breathe for itself, from deep within the heart and the abdomen. Let your shoulders drop, and have the intention to let your body breathe naturally. Pick times of the day that you are most tense and use those opportunities to pay attention to your breath. Simply stopping and noticing will change how you approach that moment. Continue to do this watchful process for as long as it takes to notice a change, a deepening and comfort, in your breathing. Don't underestimate the importance of this exercise—it is the most powerful tool you will ever learn for health and emotional peace.

Your Second Ally—A Friend of the Heart

Besides conscious breathing, what is needed at this time is at least one friend of the heart. This friend, unfortunately, often will not be your partner. The message in movies and books of couples united and strengthened through tragedy is greatly exaggerated. It does happen, but it is more common that couples will be separated by their experiences of grief and sometimes blame.

I can't emphasize enough how each individual grieves differently, and this will include your partner.

Your friend of the heart, on the other hand, will hold you in a holy place by listening intently and soulfully as you express your feelings. They won't judge you, or say you must pray your feelings away or that you're dwelling on sadness and need to move on. This person will be there in love, expecting nothing, giving their attention to your wound. He or she will know that you have to tell your story and share your emotions until you know their truth, and that takes time. Even if you have only one of these angels, you are blessed. They are your second ally on your heroic journey.

My friend Pat was that person for me. She never rushed my process. Nearly every day, after I took my kids to school, I went by her house for a hug and a cup of tea. No matter where I was in my grieving she showed me only love and patience.

Many years after Michael's death, Pat underwent surgery. I sat with her and tuned in to her heart and knew that she was receiving my love as I had received hers. Pat's unexpected death was added to my list of great losses, and my heart had a new wound, but by then I had learned to treasure the gifts she had brought to me while she was here. Her love for me, and mine for her, confirmed our souls' beauty and our connection.

John O'Donohue wrote movingly and beautifully of the *anam ċara*, translated from Gaelic as "soul friend":

The anam čara was a person to whom you could reveal the hidden intimacies of your life. This friendship was an act of recognition and belonging. When you had an anam čara, friendship cut across all convention and category. You were joined in an ancient and eternal way with the friend of your soul.

We are blessed any time we have a friend of the soul, but especially when we are struck by grief. Our emotions are all over the place, but our friend sees into our heart space. This friend, and if you're blessed there can be more than one, is an ally on the journey we must take to move through our grief and become what our souls truly desire us to be.

Grief Work: Exercise 5

Going to the Heart for an Ally

As usual, have your journal at hand as you do the next exercise. Whenever you can, leave time to write should you want to, and to just be at peace if you don't. Please use the MP3, or other music if it suits you. I find it helpful, but that's not true of everyone. Remember that there are no rules or right/wrong directions here. Your intuition will lead you.

1. Again, find a quiet place where you won't be disturbed for a little while. Put your feet flat on the floor, without shoes if possible. Close your eyes. If you need to lie down, please do so. (If you fall asleep, that's what you need.)

2. Begin once more to breathe deeply, into your heart. Breathe in through your nose and out through your nose. Count to five on the inhale and five on the exhale, taking your time, allowing your breath to become smooth and easy.

3. Gradually drop your breath to the area of your heart. If you can, see your breath the color green or pink as it bathes your heart. If another color comes, then that is right for you. Breathe.

4. Let all thoughts flow out. When you notice a new thought, let it go. We are never without our thoughts, but we can pay attention to the breath and the thoughts will slow down. Breathe deeply.

5. As you breathe deeply into your heart, experience a feeling of care or love for someone, something, or someplace in your life. Breathe the emotions of that memory into your heart. Do this for a minute or so. Feel it throughout your body. Sometimes you can hear, see, touch, or smell a place. Breathe.

6. If you have a soul friend, this is a good time to experience their presence. You can ask for any loving presence who is a guide for you to be present. Create a stronger sense of them. See, smell, touch, and hear their being or energy. As you think of them, breathe all they mean to you into your heart. Breathe in and out deeply, experienc-

ing this feeling. Take your time. After a few moments have passed, let this image fade.

7. As this image of your soul friend fades, replace it with an image of you in your heart—you as you were when you were a child. When you see yourself, send that feeling of care, of love, of appreciation that you created with the image of your soul friend to this image of your younger self. Breathe the love and appreciation into your child self from your heart.

8. Look closely at your young self and see how you are feeling. Are you sad? Was this one of those times when you were struggling? Or is this a version of you that would have the great courage to answer the call? Either way, send love and just continue to breathe in and out slowly and quietly until you can see the young you relax and melt into your heart. Breathe.

9. Open your eyes and come back into your space when you're ready.

In the future, you can ask your heart to bring up this picture of you at any age where you needed love and care, or when your adult self needs some of your younger self's courage.

What I know now is that all of our emotional responses—anger, depression, sadness, and fear—are normal and part of the heroic journey we embark on through loss. It's only when we get stuck in one of these places that we risk closing our hearts to the journey and remaining in the dark for a long time.

Sooner or later, in order to heal, we have to feel each emotion in depth, accept and allow our feelings, and move to the next level. We must give up all our usual protection, our control and safety, and go into the darkness with love and compassion. We are required to love ourselves and honor our journey. Otherwise, we will not heal, and we can't expect from others what we can't give ourselves. Courage is mandatory, but look at what we have already survived!

We are moving, always, toward growth. That is the way of the human becoming. Grief inserts itself and acts as a moving spirit to open our hearts to our highest capacities. I know it doesn't feel that way at the time. Sometimes we manage to feel nothing for a short period, but eventually our broken heart guides us to the road that leads us through and out of grief. I promise you will smile again. I promise you will think of your loss and feel peace before sorrow. That is the central gift I wish for you to find in this book.

A Gift

I promise you will one day feel peace before sorrow when you think about your loss.

If we wish to be more than survivors, then we can aspire to be creators of our own story. The question we must ask is whether or not we are ready to find the self that has not yet been birthed—the spiritual director of our lives that lives in our hearts and souls. Are we ready to see the one who is made in the crucible of our loss? It may be frightening to forge through the dark paths that lie ahead, but fear is just your small self trying to veer you off course by saying that you at least know where you are right now, and you have no idea what's ahead. But *where* you are is not meant to be *who* you are. This grief, this dark night of the soul, is to have value through directing you to your deepest places. There is a gift in the future when we can look back and see how much we have grown, how much we have honored our grief by exploring and focusing it on our soul's growth. For now, we have only faith and trust that this is true, but your heart knows for certain.

Emily Dickinson describes in these few lines how we will eventually be able to look back at such a time.

This is the Hour of Lead
Remembered, if outlived,
As Freezing persons, recollect the Snow
First—Chill—then Stupor—then the letting go.

—Emily Dickinson,
"After great pain, a formal feeling comes – (372)"

The letting go of fear is now easier for one very specific reason. We have survived a mortal wound and we are still here.

What can happen to us on this new journey that will be equal in pain to this wounding? There is no reason not to go deeper. At worst, we'll feel our pain, but at best we'll live into our god-selves—that is the greatest gift of grief. And every step is worth the journey. It's time to accept the call and begin.

> **At worst, we'll feel our pain, but at best we'll live into our god-selves—that is the greatest gift of grief.**

The work at the end of each chapter, especially the breathing, is the most valuable tool you will take with you on the journey. It is a sword to cut through doubt and a lantern to light your way to your inner knowing. Even when you have difficulty focusing, come back and try again. Think about who your allies are. Earlier in your life, had you already discovered guides and angels whose voices guide you? Are there people who died that you now feel are lending you energy when you are struggling? Ask your allies for help and fall into the rhythm of your heart and breath. It is your birthright to have these abilities. Even if your meditation practice is nonexistent or rusty, you will overcome all obstacles because the knowing comes from your heart. Have faith. Leap!

Grief Work: Exercise 6

Self-Care and Finding Allies

Don't do this exercise immediately following Exercise 5. Wait at least a few hours or, preferably, a whole day. Have your journal at hand and use music if preferred. As always, use your intuition to prepare yourself in a way that feels most comfortable to you.

1. Close your eyes and put your feet flat on the floor. If you're unable to sit, lie down.

2. Begin to breathe in through your heart, out of your heart, slowly counting to five on the inhale and five on the exhale. Breathe.

3. Let all thoughts move like clouds across the screen of your mind, eventually out of your awareness. Envision your breath expanding and contracting your heart, slowly, slowly. Be gentle with yourself and take your time.

4. Once you feel calm around your heart, fill your chest with a feeling of care and appreciation for someone, something, or someplace in your life. Breathe that in deeply, then slowly add a color to the breath. Many people use green or pink or purple; some use silver. Visualize what feels right to you, and imagine the colored breath moving in and out of your heart like a wave. See it expand and contract with each breath. Breathe deeply.

5. As you continue to relax, picture that colored breath expanding out into your whole body. Care, appreciation,

or love—whatever you have chosen—moves up your throat into your head, down into your shoulders, and through your arms down to your fingertips. Each breath is easier, and expands more deeply into your body, until you are completely filled with colored light and the feeling you have chosen.

6. Keep breathing slowly and watch as your whole body from your head to your feet breathes this colored light and becomes filled with the calm and peace of your breath.

7. Now ask your intuition and your heart to reveal another ally or allies to help you find the light on your journey through the darkness of loss. (Remember, your heart is your first ally.) Ask to see or hear the ally announce their presence.

8. If you already know your soul friend is your second ally, bring that person into your heart. Continue to breathe slowly while you wait. Give yourself as much time as you can, simply waiting quietly, breathing deeply, and feeling calm. When you are ready, open your eyes and come back into your room.

You may not see or hear a presence on the first or second practice. Just come back and do this exercise at least once a day. The relaxation and healing of the colored light will be enough. A glimpse of your ally will be a bonus gift. Write in your journal what doing this process felt like in your body. Then note any allies you met during this meditation. Also note how it felt to support your own being.

You have already entered into the darkness and seen your heart ally. And you have seen some of your enemies—your own fear, guilt, judgment, and the judgment of others. Every day is the death of who we were yesterday; it is also the birth of who we will be tomorrow if we can see our possibilities.

Every day will be different. Some days will be easier than others, but generally it gets more and more relaxing and peaceful to go to this place, and you will continue to see your allies appear. This will eventually be your personal team of guides and teachers, and you'll call upon them anytime you need information or courage to continue on your journey.

Building Your Team of Allies

I know many people who have put together a team for their spiritual healing the same way they would for work. For example, they may have a different guide for each of these categories: creativity, love, making decisions, even financial worries. They will give these guides names and sometimes see them in form. If you would like to do this, just do the meditation and ask for specific guides and teachers to show up and tell you who they are. It's a fun and amazing exercise to do when you have no expectations.

My creative guide is named Clarissa. She showed herself to me in a meditation, and I see her every day when I look ahead to my work. I expected her to be angelic with a halo of light surrounding her. Instead, she showed herself to me like a 1940s showgirl, complete with abundant red hair, flowing scarves, and the stature of a Rosetti painting crossed with Rita Hayworth. Her "tone," as in the energy that comes to me, is sometimes flippant, sometimes serious, and sometimes joyful. She is never preachy but guides me when I am fumbling in my work. Who knows what energy will show up for you? The point of this journey through the astounding abilities of our bodies, minds, and souls is not only to recover from our deepest sorrows but also to manifest our highest selves.

Sometimes we recognize the energies that present themselves to us, as I did with Michael, and other times our teachers are a complete and wonderful surprise. Just always remember to notice if their energy is in your best and highest good.

⌒

You have now discovered at least two allies on your journey. If you received guidance in the last exercise, you are blessed with protection and wisdom. Holding that truth, you are now asked to step across the threshold of fear and be fully on your journey.

Chapter 3

Overcoming Denial and Guilt

How

did the rose

ever open its heart

and give to the world all of its beauty?

It felt the encouragement of light against its being,

otherwise we all remain too

frightened.

—Hafiz, translated by Daniel Ladinsky,
"How Did the Rose?"

To stay numbed to pain, lacking empathy and compassion, is to live a very small life. Though we beg to be spared it, we cannot live in this world and expect to escape the causes of grief. To think that we will always be in perfect health, as will our parents, mate, children—even our pets—is to live according to what is called wishful or magical thinking. Children excel in magical thinking. But it isn't real. Crossing my fingers won't ensure I'll have good luck. How can we feel the "encouragement of light" spoken of by Hafiz? One of the steps is to retreat to nature. It's in nature that we feel our body respond and our heart open to the light.

There is a definite downside to living in a mechanized world. Our separation from nature allows us to put a frame around things, to see real events as if they are photographs or movies. Then we selectively edit anything we don't want to see. Our intellect is very clever this way. I see this magical thinking in people playing violent video games. "It's not real," they say, slaying the enemy right and left, watching the blood fly, believing that they are therefore protected from the effects of the games. But we know these games are modeled from real situations and create a place in the brain that *believes* it's real, releasing adrenaline and other chemicals that show the player is feeling the emotions connected with killing and maiming.

In the same mind-set, we select the surroundings of life and death, never seeing the reality of them until lightning strikes. The problem with a mind-based system is that it has no *juice*. We sort, file, label, and organize, putting our lives in little boxes, staying safe. But we can't deny the existence of the heart and soul—they will continue to remind us of their presence, and they thrive on passion and juice, the messier side of life. Just as nature explodes in mud and water and dies in sterile conditions, this messier side is where we grow. Put your bare feet down on the earth and feel. Breathe the essence of nature up into your heart and know you are not separated from Mother Earth; you are her child.

Dylan Thomas's poem "The force that through the green fuse drives the flower" is a great example of messy nature and its counterpart, human nature:

The force that through the green fuse drives the flower
Drives my green age; that blasts the roots of trees
Is my destroyer.
And I am dumb to tell the crooked rose
My youth is bent by the same wintry fever.

We see the stem of the flower, and the force (which most see as creation), but not in a sweet, slow-growing, Disney kind of way. This force drives the flower, blasts the roots of trees, and makes the rose and the writer bend in the same wintry fever. Thomas shows us our purpose as a fuse that lights us and drives us towards our spiritual destiny. And he also sees himself aging and dying like the rose, a warning that time is short and our birth contains the sureness of our death. This poem is an urgent call to notice. Native people have myths that always contain the truth of life and death, where our modern myths tend to focus on life, more life, and a search for the magic pills that will end aging.

The mind is a trickster, especially when it comes to matters of the heart and soul. The ego-mind knows it can't control you if you go off on your spiritual journey. Finding your spiritual way is never a matter of following a formula, no matter how prominent its inventor.

Grief and Society

Despite the evidence of our eyes, our brains decide that we can control our lives in a way that recreates the 1950s television shows. The biggest problem in the family is whether Mom can keep her apron clean and her feet comfy in her high heels as she whirls through the house, prepares the perfect meal, and has the perfect conversation with her perfect husband and perfect children before their perfect dessert.

Today's parents are inundated by daily bulletins from television and the Internet describing the latest fearful attack on the quality of their lives and their children's lives. Once told that deadly germs live on every surface, sending their children to day care becomes an exercise in guilt and grief. Their fears are proven right when their children come home with every kind of virus imaginable, made more virulent by the excessive use of disinfectants. In our efforts to do good and protect, we take away naturally occurring immunity. We overthink, overact, and then overreact, in an honest effort to be good parents.

At home, constant kid-centered living is an attempt to make up for what parents see as bad choices. Mothers compare themselves to their memories of the perfect stay-at-home moms of the sitcoms, a nirvana that never existed, and a contest they can't win. Meanwhile, the couple is exhausted, their relationship is on hold, and they long for a future where everything they work for will make it all right. There is a daily application of stress, and no small amount of grieving as they watch while what they think are the best years of their lives go by in a blur. If we are among those who are without a job and unable to support self or children, that is a grieving we can barely handle. To acknowledge this grief is paramount to surmounting it.

All of these attempts at control take a huge toll, including the minimal time available for joy. It's no wonder we are the most exhausted and stressed society in history. Imagine what happens in our brain when it is faced with the reality of divorce, disease, and death. It must be zipping around its storage places, looking for a rational explanation for this betrayal of years of messages.

Unexplored and denied emotions stored in the body lead to physical illness. The latest statistical data suggest that over 90 percent of doctor visits are stress related. Stress over a long period—a time where the body is releasing chemicals into our blood and bathing our cells in a toxic brew—results in multiple health issues. Anger, resentment, confusion, and lack of sleep are just a few of the symptoms of long-term stress. Many and varied diseases are now linked to stress, including high blood pressure, irritable bowel, heart issues, and some cancers. Pushing down the warning signals of stress has no basis in reality. Acknowledging our humanness and turning inward for healing, in addition to our outward actions, is the first step to wholeness.

Even if you aren't quite convinced of the physical manifestation of emotions—like sickness showing up when you're suffering grief—I ask you to suspend that disbelief long enough to try the following exercise when you can allocate about fifteen minutes to the process and some recovery time after.

Grief Work: Exercise 7

Releasing Pain

Since what we are holding is our pain, it should be a gift to let it go. I would ask you to sit quietly tonight, just before bed, and read, or preferably listen to, the following exercise on the recording. Then close your eyes, and experiment.

1. Sit with your feet flat on the floor. Close your eyes, and breathe deeply until your breathing is slow and regular. Inhale to the count of five, exhale to the count of five, feeling your chest expand and contract as you breathe.

2. Now take the breath deeper, into your abdomen (just below where your ribs come together in the middle of your body). Feel your abdomen expand on the in breath, and contract on the out breath, collapsing toward your spine. Inhale, abdomen expands; exhale, abdomen collapses. Do this several times until you are in a comfortable rhythm. Breathe.

3. Begin to add color to the breath as it flows in and out. Think of this breath as colored energy from your heart. Let the breath move throughout the body, from your chest up to your head, out through your shoulders, down your arms and out your fingers, down through your trunk, down your legs, into your feet, and out the bottoms of your feet. Feel each part of you relax as this warm, colored breath flows through you.

4. When you see that colored breath hovering just below your feet, ask your heart to tell you where the pain is stored in your body. Gradually begin to draw the breath/energy up into your feet, breathing deeply in and out as you do. Continue to breathe the energy up, carefully watching for the breath to stop and show you where the pain is stored in your cells. It will hover for a moment, sometimes vibrate, so you can feel and see the location of the pain in your body. Breathe.

5. Sometimes the pain will look a certain way—perhaps it is dark, or is a particular color. Each time the energy stops

or shows you where pain is stored, breathe deeply into that place and have the intention to release the pain. Imagine the pain as black smoke leaving your body, being replaced by the beautiful colored energy you have created. Breathe deeply as you do this.

6. Take your time and scan your whole body in this way. Be patient with yourself. You may find a little pain or a lot—you will find more each time you repeat this exercise. Each time your energy pauses, ask your heart and your other allies to show you the pain. Breathe.

7. When you feel it is time, bring the breath back to the heart, continuing to breathe deeply and slowly. When you're ready, open your eyes.

Please write in your journal after this process, and ask your allies and teachers to continue healing the pain in your body as you sleep. Write again in the morning if you sense any change that happened during sleep. Tell your truth—no one need ever see it but you.

The process of perceiving where the pain resides *physically* in your body takes some time to get used to, but you are clearly moving forward on your journey. Unless you have done this before, this is new territory of your inner self. The information provided in this book about cells, the heart, and the brain will help you adjust to the terrain of your new territory.

No Judging

I am asking you to find a place in your grieving where you can be gentle with yourself. There is no place for the harshness of judgment and blame in grief. The gifts of grief, the light in the darkness, can only enter an open heart. Grief shatters the walls built around the heart, giving light an opportunity to enter. If we glue the pieces of the heart together with anger, guilt, blame, and judgment, the darkness reigns.

Usually our worst blame and judgment are against ourselves. We always have a choice. We are allowed to choose covering up or closing off, medication or alcohol-induced numbness. We may think these ways of coping will get us around our grief, but they never work. Still, the heart allows what we desire—even if our choices are poor. Love cannot force us to its way, or it wouldn't be love. Love respects our choice, always. But for those in our lives who love us, it's hard to stand by and see our suffering. Friends and family will use their intellect to argue us into certain behaviors—for our own good. Oh, if only it were so easy, to rationalize one's way out of grief! But it's not a thinking process. The brain is not the first responder in grief—only our heart and our bodies can tell us how we *feel*.

Unresolved grief builds upon itself. . . . Even if you have embraced the popular stiff-upper-lip routine, you have a vast reservoir of built-up grief in your cells.

Keep in mind that unresolved grief builds upon itself. Loss is not limited to death—there are many little deaths throughout life. Everyone has suffered loss, from health issues or money worries to loss of a home or divorce and the vague but real loss of a dream. Even if you have embraced the popular stiff-upper-lip routine, you have a vast reservoir of built-up grief in your cells. Each event is attracted to the others, like filings to a magnet. This is why we cry when we see someone (even someone in a book or movie) suffering loss. Our empathy kicks in, yes, but so does our backlog of unshed tears.

The Science behind Pain and Grief

For generations, doctors and biologists have believed the brain is the director of the body. All memory was believed to reside in the brain, and in order to access memory, we had to access the brain. The brain sends out signals telling the body what to do, the body responds in a fight or flight, and that's that. Now we know more. For example, we know that the heart is formed in a fetus *before* the brain. The heart determines its own rhythm before the brain develops. Recent discoveries have shown that the heart contains as many neurons as certain major parts of the brain, and the heart is where we first *feel*.

And yet, those of us who were not trying to prove brain dominance always were aware of the power of the heart. We speak of it so often. "My heart is breaking." "Do it with heart." "Put your heart into it." We never forgot. The heart is not weak—it is the source of our strength and contains generations of intelligence.

It's time to turn the tables on the belief that regards our brain and its thoughts as captains of our ship. It's time to realize that our soul and body make up a completely brilliant whole-systems miracle that we inhabit. It's nice to have science back on our side, but science is only an investigative tool. We are the master musicians who can play whatever music we wish in this amazing structure we call our bodies.

The wise person realizes each of the three parts—heart, soul, and mind—must work together for us to be healthy and balanced. We have an opportunity to make that happen as we work through our grieving and prepare for the rest of our lives. Understanding how that happens will help us to embrace the exercises for healing.

The Heart-Brain Connection

We have an emotional reaction to something and it is felt in the heart—that is also where intuition is lodged. The heart communicates with the brain in several different ways. Scientists now refer to this as the heart-brain connection. According to Dr. Rollin McCraty at the Institute of HeartMath:

The heart's electrical field has forty to sixty times more amplitude than that of the brain, while the heart's magnetic field is approximately five thousand times stronger than the field produced by the brain.

Researchers have found that one of several ways the heart transmits information to the brain and to other sentient beings is via its pulsating electromagnetic field—the same technology cell phones and radio stations use. Just try imagining that! Your heart is beaming out a field of energy that can be measured eight feet or more from your body.

Doesn't this explain those feelings you have in a group, or even between two people, when one person attracts you for a warm hug and another sends you running for the door? If we are constantly sending out a field of pain and sadness, people will begin to retreat from us. If we send out a field of peace and love, people want to be in our presence. This is all a part of our beautiful intuitive body system, which includes our heart intelligence.

I believe this field is also what gives us such feelings of peace and belonging when we're in nature. My favorite cathedral in the world is Muir Woods in California. The energy and beauty of those stunning Sequoias take my breath away. On a sunny day, I look up into the crowns of the trees, a hundred or more feet above my head, and see the light pouring through. It's a purely mystical experience. I also envision the first time I snorkeled and saw the beauty of a reef and the electric-colored fish swimming so close to me. It represents a time of pure joy.

A Gift

Rediscovering nature is a natural heart response in grief. It provides us with emotional energy that nourishes us, and reminds us to feel rather than think all the time.

Energy from nature is one of the most healing energies for those who are ill or in pain—physical or emotional. When we do our healing visualizations, seeing and recalling the feelings of transcendent experiences, we flood our bodies with calming emotions. Memories of places in nature are some of the most powerful as we do the exercises that ask us to recall a peaceful or blissful time in our lives. As a licensed HeartMath provider, I've found that clients who become aware of the power of their heart-brain in tandem with their head-brain move beyond anxiety and stress into a place of peaceful knowing.

Your heart has the intelligence to take you into a new relationship with the universe. Going beyond grief is never to be confused with forgetting. We will not forget, but the painful emotional energy attached to the memory will gradually diminish if we are purposeful about removing it. Let's take a simple example.

Imagine you are walking down the street and you see a Doberman without a leash. You could feel a rush of affection if you had a Doberman you loved as a child, or fear if you were attacked by a dog as a child, or neutrality if you have no feelings whatsoever about dogs. The heart instantly reads your emotions, sending a message to the brain based on your reaction. The brain receives the heart's message, checks in with your emotional memories, and orders the autonomic nervous system and the hormone system to release the appropriate chemicals. If you like dogs, endorphins, DHEA, and other soothing hormones and chemicals put you into a state akin to love, causing your breathing to slow, your blood pressure to lower, and your heart rate to become steady and calm. In the case of fear, adrenaline, cortisol, and many other toxic chemicals are released, creating a fight-or-flight response: rapid heartbeat, flushing, quickened breathing/ shortness of breath, raised blood pressure, and sometimes a buzzing in the body.

Understanding stress also presents us with an opportunity to use our grief as the doorway to a new way of living.

Once you know the process, it is your choice whether your whole body, including all of your organs, will be bathed in toxic or healing substances. Stress is the leading cause of visits to doctors and the root of many diseases. Understanding stress also presents us with an opportunity to use our grief as the doorway to a new way of living.

Somatic Intuitive Training™

I have worked for years with a program taught by Lance Ware called Somatic Intuitive Training:

- ✦ Somatic—referring to the body's memory;
- ✦ Intuitive—finding and trusting inner resources, such as wisdom, guidance, and inspiration;
- ✦ Training—learning to replace traumatic memories.

Those who are grieving and experiencing anger, fear, regret, and other negative emotions are in a constant state of stress. That's why so many people get sick following emotionally draining events. The release of all those harmful chemicals and responses in the system creates an unhealthy situation, especially if these states last a long time. On the other hand, those who are able to learn breathing techniques, access good memories, visualize healing, and add meditation or prayer to their daily activities can directly alleviate the stress. When people get in touch with their bodies in a way that includes their heart and intuition, all healing is possible.

Biologists tell us that memory is stored in every cell of our body. It's as if we have a portable library, where everything we have ever experienced is stored. The cells are also where the connections exist with previous experiences of sadness or loss or grief. If we have not dealt with the accumulation of grief throughout our lives, we will now be asked to deal with it all at once. The good news is that we can, and the exercises we have been doing along the way are our tools. The very first step is to believe in the power of your own possibilities.

All the work we are doing in this chapter is meant to accept and acknowledge the pain our hearts are feeling. As we repeat the exercise at the beginning of this chapter, we will find that the pain lessens and we are able to continue on the journey that will transform our grief and pain into love and compassion.

A Gift

Acceptance comes after a hard-fought battle with the ego. The fact that grief has pushed us into the pain and onto the journey makes victory possible.

That is a huge gift, and one that requires not only courage, but faith in the process. Trust your heart, your ally, to take you there. Step across the threshold—you have the tools of your heart and spirit and the support of your allies. When we leave the vicinity of the mind that circles, questions, worries, and wants to know, and go to the heart where all is surety and knowing and peace, we are finding our way home.

You can begin right now to rebalance your physical body by getting in touch with where the pain is stored and using the tools in this book to remove and replace it.

Chapter 4

Healing

Prayer and love are learned in the hour when prayer becomes impossible and the heart has turned to stone.

—Thomas Merton, *Seeds of Contemplation*

One thing seems clear—though we hurt and are mourning, we want to heal. For some, leaving behind our old ways sounds so simple—just drop them off, step over them, and move on. For others, what lies ahead is a mystery and even a source of fear until we ask, what could be worse than where we are right now? However we think, if we look at these old ways one at a time, the task becomes easier. Let's take tears as an example.

The Importance of Crying

There is a sacredness in tears. They are not the mark of weakness, but of power. They speak more eloquently than ten thousand tongues. They are messengers of overwhelming grief, of deep contrition, of unspeakable love.

—Washington Irving

How many times have you swallowed your tears because you worry they are a sign of weakness or you don't want to upset others? Tears are a necessary transport for cleansing your body of the toxic results of fear, sorrow, and even anger. The fact that we have been trained to shut them off is a misguided abuse of power by individual and societal influences. Honoring grief with our tears is one of the tasks that we need to accomplish to heal ourselves. Our ability to cry reconnects us to the sacred and raises our grief from the level of the everyday to the holy ground it truly is.

When I was a child, I heard various versions of, "Stop crying, or I'll give you something to cry about." Did anyone ever think about how crazy that was? My sister laughed inappropriately at serious times, as many of us do—particularly at funerals—because the appropriate reaction of tears had been shut off by fear. Either way, the punishing parental hand was just around the corner. We can forgive the parents and the society, but we still need to reconnect to our body's natural inclination to mourn through tears.

The War of Hidden Feelings

To spare oneself from grief at all cost can be achieved only at the price of total detachment, which excludes the ability to experience happiness.

—Erich Fromm, psychoanalyst

The release that comes with tears is a gift given to us by our creator, and what a shame that we have been denied that release and rewarded for its absence. Stoic people are greatly admired in our world. It's been our society's way of being for centuries. One example that is still relevant today is the soldiers who come back from war with horrific wounds, both to their physical bodies and to their psyches, and are admired for their cheerful countenance and can-do attitudes. Meanwhile, on the inside, their bodies are busy fighting another war—the war of hidden feelings.

Suicide levels for soldiers returning from Iraq and Afghanistan are heartbreaking. In 2011, a veteran died by suicide every eighty minutes, according to a report from the Center for a New American Security. By June 2012, more soldiers had died by suicide than in action in Iraq and Afghanistan combined. This sends not only a message but also energy of great sadness and fear onto the planet. This is part of what I term global, or universal, grief.

Grieving takes up a huge amount of body and soul energy, whether it be the loss of a limb in battle, the loss of mobility through illness, or the particular loss of a parent, spouse, child, family member, or friend. If we add to that the burden of learning to hide our feelings and our pain, we are overwhelming the body's ability to heal. We can have a warrior spirit and still need time to cry and mourn. To suffer in silence only adds to our grief. The first few times that we coax our tears to come out of hiding can be truly shocking. We may experience a small rivulet of tears down our cheek or we may experience a wracking, painful breaking apart in our chest or throat and an avalanche of sobs. Or somewhere in between. Tears are not increasing our burden or our loss. They are not a sign of weakness; they are merely a vehicle for expressing our grief. As John O'Donohue, a beautiful writer, counselor, and philosopher, said in his poem "On the Death of the Beloved":

Though we need to weep your loss,
You dwell in that safe place in our hearts,
Where no storm or night or pain can reach you.

Be patient with yourself as you try the next exercise. It may take a while for you to melt the ice built up over time.

Grief Work: Exercise 8

Releasing Tears

If your heart is touched by music, and you don't have the MP3 "The Gifts of Grief Meditations," I recommend several CDs or pieces in the resources section.

1. Make yourself as comfortable as possible. Close your eyes. Begin to breathe in quietly and slowly—into your heart, out of your heart. Be aware of your shoulders—are they tense or relaxed? What about your arms and hands? Are your hands lying softly in your lap, fingers open loosely, or are they rigid and clenched? Check your whole body and breathe deeply into each part of it until it is relaxed. Breathe.

2. When your body is relaxed, go back into your heart, breathing deeply in and out. Ask for any guides or allies who wish to join you to come now, forming a ring of protection and support around you. See and sense their energy as they arrive. Breathe.

3. Now imagine your heart surrounded by an emerald glow of light. Deepen the color and, as you breathe in and out, say the word "love" to yourself and observe as the color around your heart begins to glow like a vivid green flame.

4. Now have the intention to strengthen your awareness of the allies surrounding you in this space. Ask them to help you as you contact the loving feelings and your feelings of loss and grief. Breathe.

5. Now go to your grief—see it, hear it, sense it in any way that you believe your grief would look. Place that picture of grief in the green flame of your heart. Just breathe this time of grief in and out of your heart slowly and peacefully for a time. Just breathe.

6. Ask your body if it would be willing to release the grief inside your heart in the form of visible, warm salty tears or in any other way that feels right to you. After you ask, sit quietly and wait for the answer. Breathe.

7. If your body is not ready and refuses to cry, let it go. This is not the time. Send love and gratitude to your heart and your body. They have suffered much.

8. Watch the picture of grief disappear into the green flame and then simply thank your heart, your allies, and your body for being willing to try. Plan to come back to this another time. Breathe in peace and calm.

9. Sit quietly and breathe in and out slowly until you are ready to open your eyes and come back into your space.

Write about this in your journal. If you were unable to release your tears, ask yourself, and your guides, what blocks you. Take your time and try again later.

The Gifts of Grief

I'd like to close this section with one last poem about the beauty of tears:

The
Heart is right to cry
Even when the smallest drop of light,
Of love,
Is taken away. . . .

But you are so right
To do so in any fashion

Until God returns
To
You.

—Hafiz, translated by Daniel Ladinsky, "The Heart Is Right"

How different is the poet's approach to life from the way we have learned from a very young age? Earlier we covered all the modern ways that we fight against anything we see as different or scary. But it's a long way from acceptance to inviting in the fearsome happening and being grateful. How difficult will it be for us to leave behind our old ways of thinking in order to move forward on this new path, opened by our grief? It will depend on how prepared we are to follow the path deep into our journey and recognize our gifts.

Now that we have accessed some of our guides and allies, we can continue to do the exercises on a daily basis. Our new routine of practicing our exercises creates a sense of protection and safety. When we see ourselves as the knight in search of the gifts as opposed to the one who is at grief's mercy, the challenges will be met with courage and results. Our path may not be a straightforward one; we'll be all over the place, and some days will be better than others. We'll travel through our journey erratically, back and forth between steps, up and down in our emotions, in the presence or absence of tears. It doesn't matter. We are moving forward every day. We are on a quest where very little of the future is seen. We are traveling on faith and receiving our gifts as we go. We are capable of anything, but must listen deeply to our inner knowing.

As we open ourselves to this inner voice, what would be the gifts you would look for if you were able to choose? Some of us desire peace, some an understanding and a growth in our spirituality, and others desire to turn this experience into life changes that will make our grieving assume a purpose. Many of the gifts received as we enter the light of our own truth are unexpected. Others are desires of our heart and soul. Each of you must choose—and there may be more than one choice for you.

You Are Not Your Grief Story

I have clients who have been telling their story to others, including therapists, for years. They are filled with anger, regret, and blame. Sometimes their anger is so intense it will flow over to me as I encourage them to leave the story behind. They wonder who they will be without their story.

In the beginning, we must tell our story, particularly to our friend or friends of the heart. But soon, that story begins to take up residence in the cells and becomes the answer to "who are you?" We are not our darkest story. We are our heart, our soul, our relation to the earth, the people on the earth, and our relationship with ourselves. We are teachers, healers, parents, siblings, daughters and sons, friends and lovers. We are so many things that to narrow ourselves down to the angry or disappointed or grieving self of our story is to deny our God-given beauty.

So, yes, some of us will tell our story over and over, particularly if it is a grief beyond our understanding. Telling it leads to some small amount of comprehension. But the story of our grief is only a small part of us. If we allow it to take up permanent residence throughout our body, mind, and spirit we will have a lot of work to do in the darkness. So what is the alternative? We must tell ourselves it's time to make a conscious choice for healing, knowing in our hearts that we will be supported. In

that gift we will rediscover the holiness and beauty of life—and
death.

A Gift
**We will go from living little lives to living
lives of purpose and meaning.**

Simply put, making the choice to heal sets our feet on the
path. The rest of the journey will unfold at its own pace, and
contains many surprises—just like life.

No Grief Too Small

In my own world, I often find that something sneaks up on me
that was not included in the work I have done on my own grieving. There were times when moments of grief were revealed to
me but I belittled them. It has been a long road for me to discover that the accumulation of small- and medium-sized betray-
als equals large amounts of stored grief. I began my spiritual
work as an uninformed normal human being who thought that
if it was spiritual, important, or worth addressing it had to be
big. I am humbled by how much I have learned over the years
about how everything, no matter how small, has importance.

Remember how we talked earlier of the illness that frequently follows a major—or even minor—shock to our sys-

tems? The grieving possibilities listed at the beginning of the book can all produce sickness in the body during and after. Other life experiences, such as having our house invaded, our purse snatched, or even what seems like an uneventful fall, can lead to problems with our health. Making the choice to be aware and always use our heart tools will keep us healthy in the midst of the chaos that life sometimes brings. Some of the heart tools you have been learning are: changing the way you breathe; bathing the heart in light; doing the exercises; reconnecting your heart with nature; and transforming pain through the heart.

A Crisis of Faith

A client was referred to me who suffered from severe physical issues whose cause modern medicine had been unable to diagnose. Her doctor sent her to a therapist, yet any suggestion that grief was connected to her physical symptoms was met with denial and anger directed at the therapist. Her denial was attached to fear. She was devout in her religious faith, and "God's will" was her mantra. She insisted that she was comfortable with her losses as she had practiced the acceptance of God's will her entire life. She felt that if she questioned now, her house of belief would crumble around her, and, according to her beliefs, she would stand alone and without protection.

This is a common misconception. Many of us are raised in faith communities that ask us to accept that everything has a purpose. We can go on for years with this shining belief buoying us in our daily lives until our grief, sometimes built over the years of smaller griefs, becomes unbearable and we think we have to choose between our belief system and our emotions. This is rarely true. Believing that life has a purpose or even that everything is directed by our vision of God doesn't protect us from human emotions. Denying our grief stores all our feelings deep in the body where they lie in wait. Not expressing or exploring these feelings doesn't mean they aren't there. Sooner or later these deeply buried emotional seeds grow into plants that demand to be tended. It is here that those who fear a loss of faith if they acknowledge their body's messages make an uninformed either-or choice. They have yet to learn that holy people are wholly human.

St. Irenaeus said, "The glory of God is a human being fully alive." If this is so, and I believe that it is, we must allow all of our emotions—from the joyful to the sad—to express through us. There are other basic physical reasons for doing this—our reasons are not always spiritual. Grieving isn't just the process of releasing these pent-up emotional stresses; it is also a process of gathering sorrow from the mind/body and placing it in the heart, where love creates healing.

When someone near to us experiences a grievous loss, it is as if they took the fall. They are a lightning rod that protects us from our own tragedy. When the lightning finally hits us, we are simply not prepared for the shock. Deep in our heart and soul, we know that all of our efforts to protect and project have failed. Can you feel the enormous amount of energy we expend in trying to avoid suffering? It is time now—time to go into the pain, not around it. It is time to see what our pain is made of.

Grief Work: Exercise 9

Releasing Sorrow and Accepting Compassion

Listen to the MP3, or read this carefully.

1. Close your eyes and begin breathing deeply.

2. See your heart, and fill it with feelings of love and peace by breathing deeply and finding a place of love as you've done before. Breathe.

3. Picture your sorrow as a thing—a living thing crying for attention in your body. See it as a dark color—grey, black, or brown. Breathe.

4. Visualize putting your physical hands on this living vision of sorrow. Send words and feelings of love and forgiveness to the overwhelming sadness you've been feeling. Take as long as you need, breathing deeply, feeling the music.

5. Now ask the sorrow to collect, physically, in your heart. Picture the sorrow changing color as it travels and see it lighten as it's embraced in the heart by love, peace, and acceptance. What color is it now? Rose? Green? Purple? Blue? See it in your heart. Breathe deeply into the sorrow, into the heart.

6. Imagine your sorrow being absorbed into the love in your heart. Feel your heart expand with love and compassion for you and the sorrow you've endured, and watch as the sorrow becomes part of the light of your heart's love.

7. Now feel that love and compassion spreading out into your whole body with each beat of your heart. Visualize the color as it vibrates into every cell. Take your time. This is very sacred work.

8. When you're ready, open your eyes.

Write about this visualization in your journal. Repeat this visualization as often as you feel called to do so until you have transformed your sorrow into peace.

The journey through life, like the journey through grief, becomes a totally different trip when taken in love and compassion instead of fear, anger, and judgment. Eventually, the rest of our life will be created from the emotional intentions, choices, and compassionate heart that we have learned to heed through this long journey.

Explore Unexpected Talents to Support You through Grief

Do I contradict myself?

Very well then I contradict myself,

(I am large, I contain multitudes.)

—Walt Whitman, "Song of Myself"

For me, poetry is a saving grace. For others, coming to some understanding of feelings is possible through music, woodworking, painting, knitting, meditation or prayer, and a host of other things. Step out of your box. Try something new to express yourself, and this will be another gift you've discovered on the journey through grief. Don't even think about failure—when I painted my first picture I hid it for quite a while. When I took it out, it eventually became the cover for a book. Being in the grieving place can stimulate things deep inside that we don't even know are there, and we often use those to express our grief in ways that come as a complete surprise.

To think of dancing or playing music is beyond possibility for many when grief's darkness has lowered itself upon us, but I promise you it won't always be this way. I would never have believed it was possible to move from my shock at hearing music on the day of Michael's death to using heart-centered music to create my visualization CD, *The Promise: Walking Your Path of Truth,* in 2006. Now all of my deadened senses have come to life, and come to life with a stronger connection to the being and work of others.

I had never painted in my life, but after my divorce I was taken over by a part of me I'd never experienced before, an inner ally called *the creative.* I named her Clarissa, and I call upon this part of myself whenever I need creative assistance. I used painting as an outlet for my emotions. While I was painting, the grief was washing onto the canvas. The same goes for when I write. If I am writing poetry, the grief is vibrating on the page.

It's through my poetry that I am able to process the thoughts that appear in my grief, and it would be devastating if I didn't have a way to express them in a healthy (albeit sometimes painful) way. For instance, "Delicate Balance" is a poem I wrote about the rituals of staving off disaster, especially when we have children who are no longer safe at home, but out in the world that parents fear. This poem shows the underlying fear that comes at the sound of an ambulance—someone is in trouble, we pray it is not us, and yet we feel sorrow for whoever it is. (Isn't that what we do? We don't want to wish sorrow on others, but by saying not me, not me, that is exactly what we are doing.) It's these fears that cause us to overreact, overparent, and overprotect our loved ones. These are the fears that prompt us to clean our grocery cart with disinfectant, lock the car doors when we see someone standing at the street corner, or feel guilt in sending our children to day care.

But now it is time to let go of what we are holding on to that holds us down. We must learn to let go of the things we hold on to the most tightly; especially the ones that cause us pain. Step one is to release the dark weight from our bodies.

Grief Work: Exercise 10

Access Your Anger

Our bodies are amazing energy workers for us, and we often don't even realize it. In this exercise you will learn how to anchor your feelings. This is a practice that should be done daily—ideally, more than once a day.

1. Sit comfortably and close your eyes. Bring into your heart and around your body all of the guides, teachers, and allies you have discovered so far on this journey. Also ask for any protective angels or other mentors that have only your highest and best at heart to surround you now. When you're ready, begin the process.

2. Recall a time when you were really angry with someone. Don't be afraid of anger—releasing it will heal more than your body. Imagine the setting, their behavior, and what caused your anger. Now imagine yourself in the scene and feel your anger. If it feels right, in the scene

you can raise your voice—this is your imagination working, after all. Silently, in your mind, tell them exactly how their behavior made you feel. Tell them everything that comes up around this incident. Breathe.

3. When you're finished and have no more to say, put your attention on your body. What is your breathing like? Where is your breath coming into and going out of your body? Is it high in your chest, in your heart, or in your abdomen? Is it short or long? Fast or slow? What does your body feel like? Is your face tense? Your shoulders? How does your stomach feel? Are your hands relaxed or in fists? Take your time and notice all of the feelings in your body.

4. Return to noticing your breath and let the scene fade away. Slow down your breath. Breathe deeply into your heart, slowly, gently—long, deep breaths. Slow down. Let your hands rest softly in your lap. Relax your shoulders. Breathe deeply, slowly.

5. Now remember a time when you were grateful, peaceful, or loving. Bring that memory to life and make sure the other memory has faded away completely. Breathe in the smells, feelings, and emotions of this good memory into your heart. Continue to breathe deeply into this loving memory for a minute or so. Breathe.

6. Notice how your body feels as you breathe in this gentle, loving memory. Where is your breath? Where are your shoulders? Are your hands loose or tense in your lap? Notice the difference. Take your time. Breathe.

7. Would you like to anchor this feeling in your body to use anytime you want to? If so, sit quietly with the

grateful, peaceful, or loving feeling. Put the pads of your thumb and forefinger of your left hand together lightly, feeling the energy between them. Do the same with your right hand. Breathe.

8. Continue to breathe deeply into and out of your heart.

9. Now take the energy that's in your heart—the emotional energy of peace, love, and calm—and imagine it going down your arms and into the place where your fingers are touching.

10. As you send that energy down into your fingers, count backwards slowly and silently from ten down to one, deepening the feeling with each number. You are anchoring this feeling so you can use it later. Call this anchor peace and calm.

11. When you finish that process, release your fingers and breathe deeply into and out of your heart. When you're ready, open your eyes.

Immediately after you've finished the exercise, note the physical reactions of your body to the anger piece and then to the love and gratitude piece. Record every detail you can. Also write what it felt like to anchor the feelings. You will see how healthy the positive emotions are and how damaging the negative emotions are. Your body always gives you the answers.

It's important that you see the differences presented in your physical body by simply focusing on these positive and negative emotions. The experiment was to see how the thoughts in the mind and the emotions created by the thoughts affect the body. Can you see by the two different experiences—anger and peace, the brain and the heart—what showed up in your breathing and relaxation of your body? The first is what stress does to us. The second is what we can do to reverse those symptoms. When our breath gets short and our muscles tense and our heart pounds, all of the chemicals of stress are being released into our bodies. These chemicals and our reactions create opportunities for illness and disease through several routes—one being a lowering of our immune system. When we're in the midst of a stress-filled situation, simply adopting the one tool of putting attention on the heart and breathing through the heart lowers the possibility of damage to the body.

Now that you have practiced accessing your tears, taking your ego thoughts to the heart, and anchoring your emotions, you are well on your way to understanding the physical and emotional aspects of healing. It's not possible to go on this journey without an understanding of the body and its participation in grieving. We are not trying to go around our grief, but enter it and transform it to a way of life that is meaningful. Remember that in every heroic journey, our heroes don't run from their villains but rather face them head on—and it's through this confrontation that they are able to emerge as victors on the other side.

Anchoring

In the last exercise, I took you through an anchoring technique to help you store the steps deep into your cellular structure. We do this without awareness thousands of times during our life—this is called unconscious anchoring, while the anchoring we just did is conscious.

For instance, if you feel warm and nostalgic when you hear a certain song, it's because you anchored it in your body when you first heard it and felt certain emotions—it might have been your first dance with a boyfriend or girlfriend, at your wedding, or while driving along a country road and feeling at one with nature. Whatever it was, when you hear that song it recreates and re-anchors those good feelings.

Smells are some of the strongest anchors, whether pleasant or unpleasant. The scent of apples may bring back a time when you picked apples as a child or went into your first apple barn with family and were overwhelmed with the scent and the emotion of being in that moment. For the rest of your life, the smell of an apple will bring back that memory and the emotion connected with it. Sometimes you will just feel the emotion and the memory will be gone. On the other hand, if you worked in a factory that made applesauce from sunrise to sunset every day, the smell of apples may cause you to have feelings that are less than nostalgic.

For me, the smell of peonies or lilacs returns me to my childhood in Illinois and also the beauty of my personal May altar I constructed each year in the bedroom. The scent of those flowers takes me to the emotions of love and belonging and the beauty of spring. The smell of camphor reminds me of being shut indoors with asthma in the winter and rouses feelings of melancholy.

In this book, anchoring is used consciously to instill in the body feelings of peace, love, and power. We did this using various fingers as the site of the anchor so that we can bring them back at will. Anchoring is a process you will need to practice. Daily, especially morning and night, touch the fingers together and revisit that place of peace and calm. Practicing your anchor throughout the day will strengthen it until you reach the point where just touching those fingers together brings you into a peaceful, calm space. Then, you can use the anchor by touching those fingers together when you are going into any situation that could be less than peaceful, like a conversation at home or at work or simply entering a space that you know has negative energy.

⌒

Joan Halifax, author, Buddhist teacher, and hospice caregiver, summed up the journey of trials so well in her book *Being with the Dying*: "Catastrophe is the essence of the spiritual path, a series of breakdowns allowing us to discover the threads that weave all of life into a whole cloth." This weaving of a new life is one of the gifts of grief, and one I hope you are approaching if you haven't yet seized it. The tapestry you'll weave with all the threads of this journey will be as beautiful as Joseph's coat of many colors.

A Gift
Creating a new life from the pieces of your old one is a priceless gift of grief.

Another of my favorite poets, William Stafford, passed away several years ago but left a legacy of heart writing and kindness that will always be treasured. His life was full of pain and sorrow, but he had another way of seeing the healing process. He summed it up in a few words that I have in front of me every day: "I have woven a parachute out of everything broken."

Weaving seems to be one of the favorite images for healing our brokenness. Our personal parachute will bring us safely down to the ground of our new time and space. I hope that at some point in this healing process you, too, will be led to write about the images and healings that have come alive in your visualizations and journaling.

Chapter 5

Compassion

There are two ways to live your life. One is as though nothing is a miracle. The other is as though everything is a miracle.

—Albert Einstein

When making a place for forgiveness, perspective is everything.

When my son died, I was thirty-two years old and my husband was only a few years older. No one I knew could have suggested to me that I take my sorrow into my heart, let alone that I could learn how to teach this process to others. If anyone was doing grief work, it was under the radar.

I went once to a group in my church. They gathered around me with faces alight with joy and asked me the questions the grieving cannot bear, "Aren't you happy that he's with Jesus in heaven?" My heart cried out, "No! I want him here with me."

They were asking me to put on a happy face in the midst of my deep longing for the presence of my son. They were asking me to deny that every morning I awoke hoping he was in his room getting ready for school, not under the ground. Yet how could I tell these well-meaning people my pain when they were comfortable asking that question? I did all the things I am asking you not to do—I buried my son every day by not speaking my truth and healing through looking at and transforming my emotions.

It's important to remember that my perspective at that time in my life and the grief and sadness I felt were valid. It was not about saying I was wrong to feel as I did but to forgive those things that needed forgiving so I could move on, lighter and more compassionate. Compassion is a gift to be found in grief that is only available once we open to a spiritual perspective of our physical lives.

A Gift

Compassion and forgiveness are our companions as we move through grief. They won't disappear when we are healed.

Most importantly, please don't judge your feelings as "bad." We are so skilled at blaming ourselves or others. Forgiveness is for us, for our growth, and for helping us be more of who we are on the loving and compassionate side of life. It's not forgetting but clearing the space in our inner world that has been occupied with blame, anger, and regret. Forgiving creates a wonderful lightness of being.

Forgive those things that need forgiving so you can move on, lighter and more compassionate.

It's necessary to be conscious of the way we store events in the body and how they create layers of similar emotions—grief with grief, joy with joy, anger with anger, and love with love. These layers are like the strata in rocks, building great cliffs of emotions that are touched each time another similar emotion is experienced. A recent sadness gathers into it all the sadness previously stored in the body. This requires a concentrated excavation effort.

For example, many marriages are impacted by people from the past. Our spouse says something totally neutral, yet we go into a rage or a place of sadness or suddenly feel attacked. What happened? Most often, if we are female, our mate has repeated something said to us by our father or first husband or mentor of some kind that impacted us very negatively. When our mate spoke, the words resonated with the times in our lives we heard those same words in a negative way. This is also true of men and the female triggers from their past. Our past comes up to be seen, and healed, through our current relationship.

That is one of the gifts of relationship—it shows us where we need to work.

Since we have accepted the call to undertake our heroic journey and have surrounded ourselves with allies, each time we enter our bodies to discover what else we have stored there, we have protection. Also, we now know these stored emotional memories are opportunities for growth.

As author Pema Chödrön says: "Nothing ever goes away until it has taught us what we need to know." This is true of grief and true of every incident that has occurred in our lives where we had an emotional reaction. We store each of those memories in our cellular body and have our lifetime to access, understand, and either remove or change our understanding of these memories. They will not go away until we have addressed them and learned what we need to know. The good news is that once we've accessed one grief memory, we can access all of them.

> Nothing ever goes away until it has taught us
> what we need to know.

Discovering My Grief

As a young woman born and raised in Illinois, I experienced separation from friends and neighborhood as my parents moved—twice in five years. The first time, our family moved from the urban community that I was born into that included my grandparents, aunts, uncles, and cousins, and a real sense of where I came from and where I belonged. As I was going into seventh grade in my small Catholic school, which I'd entered at five, my parents moved us to the country. My father decided to show us how to live the rural life, which included learning how to use tools and raise animals. He said it was so we wouldn't grow up spoiled, but we were far from that.

Removed from everything familiar, it took me years to adapt and adjust. My siblings and I had helped build a modern home over the bones of an old house with a well, no plumbing, and asbestos shingles. We lived in the basement as we demolished the old and began the new. Once we got the plumbing in, we picked a night to burn the outhouse down. Fire departments came from three counties. It's hard for me to remember how humiliating that was as a teenager. It was not the way I wanted to meet my new community.

I never grieved that move because it was the 1950s and everyone did what they were told without question—even my mother. It was only as I grew older that I understood what that move meant to her and her roots. Meanwhile, I adapted. After all, I told myself, it had turned out well in the long term.

Then, just before my senior year, my dad moved us to Florida. I went from a class of twenty-one, which included my friends and my boyfriend, to a sophisticated South Florida high school with 350 strangers in my class. I was terrified. But I didn't grieve. What was there to grieve when my home was new and beautiful and the sun shone every day? It would have been ungrateful, and I had long practiced the habit of being thankful for what I had. However, that thankfulness doesn't matter when there are grief and separation at the forefront.

What was I storing in my body besides fear and teen angst in those blocks of frozen tears? There was anger over my lack of control over my life, and guilt resulting from that anger. I was painting a picture of myself as a whiner and someone who didn't appreciate the life that I had. This secret image would come back to haunt me for years in the form of low self-esteem.

Being moved at those two points in my life—two ages so important to social adaptation—had a huge impact on me, my siblings, and my parents. Using the exercises in this book, I have allowed the girl I was to go through the process of understanding the pain and healing it. Part of my healing path is to go back and imagine my parents as they were at that time and imagine what their thought process was. My dad was finally, in his late thirties, breaking away from his own parents when we moved to the farm. He was choosing a way that was opposed to everything his father wanted from him. Seeing him at that age was eye- and heart-opening. Knowing that he had served in the war, come home to a family business, a long-ingrained family dynamic, and the responsibilities of children and a wife gave me a new perspective and put me in a place of compassion where I could forgive, but it also gave me the capacity to admire his courage.

As I did with my father's decision to move our family from a place of safety and long-term understanding, we can look with new eyes, create a new perspective, forgive, and release negative thoughts. All of these are energetic transfers from the negative, gloomy, judgmental perspectives that are draining the life from our bodies to new perceptive, creative, hopeful, and compassionate packages of energy that light us up.

Surprisingly, lots of people have become so enraptured with holding on to the draining emotions of hate, anger, judgment, resentment, and blame for such a long time that it has become the story of the body. These old ways of being fight to exist through the ego. But now, we have simple tools that will show the ego how much healthier we can be through accepting new information and storing that energy in our cells.

Everyday Compassion

As I was writing this section, the phone rang. My friend had been struggling with a difficult issue, and she launched into a long, angry tirade. I started to tell her I had to cut her short since I was working, when it hit me. This was a real-life opportunity to practice what I teach—be patient, listen, put myself in her place, and have compassion for what she was going through. Now was not the time to talk to her about her story. That would have been useless in her current place. What she needed was a friend of the heart to just listen and offer to be there. It was another reminder that we aren't operating in a huge arena of operatic-sized angst and grief. Daily we operate in the world of little grievances and little dramas. Silently I said the prayer I love from A Course in Miracles:

Every decision I make is a choice between a grievance and a miracle.

I relinquish all regrets, grievances and resentments and I choose the miracle.

My body relaxed, my ego stepped aside, and I chose to expect the miracle. And as if on cue, my friend said: "But you know what? I almost forgot to tell you about my victory today I was so focused on the negative. Thank you!"

"Thank you?" I hadn't done a thing but listen and change my energetic perspective from judgment to compassion. She felt my energy move from brain to heart without me saying anything—a demonstration of how our energy impacts others, even over the phone. Imagine how powerful it is in person.

Opening to Compassion

One of the greatest gifts of grief is the opening of our hearts and bodies to the knowing that others are suffering. How is it possible we could have not known or felt the others who suffer as much as we do before our grief? In spite of television bringing to us stories of starvation, massacres, wars, and endless suffering of others, most of us only experience surface sympathy. Now that we have experienced loss and sadness, we have moved into empathy. And this empathy crosses over onto those who do not show their losses.

A Gift

Experiencing grief leads us to have greater empathy for others.

For myself, I am aware now of how many people in this very moment, all over the planet, are being visited by an unthinkable tragedy. I never thought about this quite the same before my great loss. When I'm on the road and see an accident off to the side, or I'm held up in traffic with red lights blinking far ahead, I immediately start to pray for those who are experiencing that river of before and after. I am so aware of how their life is changing in the moment. Around me, people fidget, walk, curse, and honk. I know they have yet to fully acknowledge their personal mudslide of loss. This doesn't mean they haven't experienced losses in their lives, it just means that they have buried those experiences so deeply they can't feel compassion or empathy for what others are going through at this time.

I have loved the poetry of Miller Williams for many years, and his poem "Compassion" never leaves my heart.

Have compassion for everyone you meet
even if they don't want it. What seems conceit,
bad manners, or cynicism is always a sign
of things no ears have heard, no eyes have seen.
You do not know what wars are going on
down there where the spirit meets the bone.

How true is this observation? How true is it about you, as you go about the business of life? How many people can tell by looking at you what you have endured? Sometimes being unable to act the way society expects is misinterpreted as bad manners. Hold this in your heart when you make a judgment about someone. We never know.

From the beginning of recorded time we have learned that it is a human trait to put ourselves in another's place, or to experience that fellow feeling. The process of going to the heart in grief makes us deeply aware of the compassionate side of us.

The ego will ask why the person or situation may not have the same empathy with us, but that is irrelevant. What matters is what builds in your heart and creates a place of understanding. It begins one person at a time, and our energy will radiate out to others and touch them in a way that may awaken the compassionate side of their hearts. Whether it does or not, you have the gift to affect others with your emotions.

Grief Work: Exercise 11

Sending Compassion

You will be setting an anchor, as you did in Exercise 10.

1. Sit with your feet flat on the floor. Be in a place where you will be undisturbed and peaceful. Notice the location of your breath. Relax your shoulders, and scan your body for any tension. When you find it, release it.

2. Bring your breath into your heart. If you like, color the breath a peaceful shade—usually green or pink. Breathe in the feelings of peace and calm. Touch your fingers together to stimulate the anchor of peace and calm.

3. Now inhale deeply through your heart and find a time and place where you felt great compassion for someone or something. Breathe. Find compassion. On the inhale, breathe in compassion. On the exhale, drop your breath into your abdomen and exhale compassion out of your

abdomen into your space. Continue to do this for about one minute. Breathe.

4. Think of an individual or place on the planet that needs your compassionate energy. Using your intuition, ask your guides and teachers for information about this person or place. Continue to breathe in and out until you hear the answer to your question.

5. On the exhale begin to send that beautiful breath of compassion out into your room, through the roof, and on to anyone or anything you feel needs compassion at this particular time. Breathe.

6. Continue to breathe deeply, sending and receiving compassion from your heart, out through your abdomen, and back into your heart.

7. When you feel you have spent all the time you can, bring the breath back into your heart, breathing deeply in and out. Thank your heart for its ability to feel and project compassion, and feel gratitude for your ability to connect energetically with other beings or places.

8. To anchor this feeling of compassion so you can come back to it anytime, lightly put together your thumb and ring finger on each hand. The ring finger, for me, represents love and compassion, which is why I use it for this exercise. Now count slowly back from ten to one, sending this feeling of compassion into the energy of the touching fingers. When you have stored the feelings of compassion in your fingers, relax your hands. Continue to breathe deeply in a place of peace and compassion.

9. When you're ready, come back to the room.

Please write in your journal and note the location of your anchor for compassion. Use the anchor every day, morning and night at a minimum, until it becomes strong and brings the feeling of compassion immediately as you touch the fingers together. When you are entering a meeting or conversation—whether at work or in relationship—you can hold these fingers together without anyone noticing.

Embracing the Unknown

One thing to remember as we go through our daily routines is that we have places in our hearts that are unknown to us. Into this unexpected territory comes grief, forcing us to look deeper. The journey into this unexplored continent reveals parts of us we never knew existed. The courageous will discover how truly magnificent are our hidden valleys and deep rivers. We'll also find parts of us that we will judge harshly because we've been taught to cover up all things dark and suspect—like anger, judgment, and suspicion. If we give ourselves permission to embrace all parts of us, freedom arises. This is similar to embracing nature. We know the scary parts exist—we've seen them on the National Geographic channel. Though we don't want to come face to face with a cobra, an orca, or a rattlesnake, we can still recognize their place in the big picture. It's the same with the parts of our human landscape. We may see our anger or resentment as dark and ugly, but both are integral emotions that we have a right to feel and that point out where we need to go to do our work.

If we give ourselves permission to embrace all parts of us, freedom arises.

One of the major gifts I received many years after losing my son was the training and openness to learn and teach others the power of grief to change one's life. For example, if we use our heart tool—going to our heart and breathing—before responding to someone in anger or fear, we will consciously choose to respond without blame or judgment. When I got angry with the people who asked, "Aren't you happy Michael's in heaven?" I came from judgment. "How could they do that?" But now, as I put that question into my heart space, I have a more compassionate answer. They *didn't* know how I felt. They may have even feared to know the feeling and went to the safe place of religion and spoke the words that my hurting heart rejected. The problem arose when I judged and rejected them. I don't blame myself for that—I was not where I am now in my understanding of compassion, intention, and choice, and even being here I will often fail to be compassionate in the moment. Sometimes it takes me a while to give over to my heart.

Never doubt that the open, compassionate heart is a strong heart.

I never doubt that the open, compassionate heart is a strong heart. The closed and angry heart is weak and will show a lack of coherence or energy when tested. But this knowing came to me as one of my gifts on the journey through my grief. As Doc Childre, founder of HeartMath, puts it: "At the speed of life today, operating with low heart energy is often compared to a vehicle that's operating low on oil, which increases the vulnerability to stress and malfunction."

Chapter 6

Intention

Your vision will become clear only when you can look into your own heart. Who looks outside, dreams; who looks inside, awakens.

—Carl Jung

The latest findings of science—especially quantum physics and biology—have shown that the intention of the experimenter determines the result. In other words, our intentions determine what road we will choose to embark on in our mortal and spiritual life—or, in the case of science, whether we will see an energy wave or a particle. With the misunderstanding of intention that comes from these experiments, people feel free to ask why we aren't moving on or getting over our grief if all we have to do is intend it.

A lot has been said about the power of intention, and much

of it is confusing, dogmatic, and sometimes misleading. In our personal and spiritual life, intention cannot come from the ego. The ego asks for things such as a big, new house, a certain amount of money, a way of being that makes everyone else comfortable, or a way to escape the lessons of life. When our intention is sent from a place of love and connection with the universe—a place of selflessness—we have a better chance of manifesting what is meant for our soul's growth. For us, it means manifesting a place where our grief becomes converted into energy to fulfill our life's purpose.

A Gift
Fulfilling our life purpose would be the greatest gift to arise from grief.

Our intention is to experience the world as a place where we connect with others in the desire for peace, love, and health. If, for example, we focus on what we see as negative qualities in our partner, we will develop negative qualities ourselves such as judgment, criticism, and resentment simply by focusing our attention on the negative. On the other hand, if we focus on our partner's positive features, we develop positive qualities such as compassion, empathy, and loving-kindness. Either we create a dysfunctional partnership based on fault and division, or we create a partnership that seeks to build a spiritual purpose based on love and respect. We can all think of relationships that reflect these two types of dynamics. By placing our focus on positive or negative aspects of a person or situation, we start to develop similar qualities in ourselves. We must work to make conscious decisions about what we choose to focus our intention on.

Sometimes the partnership is beyond repair and though we look through our hearts and our compassion, our intuition says we are both better off making other choices. A spiritual partnership can't exist with only one person moving towards it. We cannot intend a partnership to change on our own since our partner will have his or her own intentions. We can, however, intend compassion as we remake our life.

Have the Courage to Forgive Others

As our energy changes, we will see change in those around us. Some will become closer, but be prepared for those who live in fear to leave. They do not know the you that is being born. The loss of certain people in our lives, even when it's for our own good, still creates a state of grief. It can be minimal or much larger, depending on the duration and intensity of the relationship. We need to learn to let go of those who desire to break contact with the new self that is being born in us. These lessons will later be recognized as gifts.

Grief Work: Exercise 12

Forgiving and Letting Go of Others

Remember that relationships that need forgiving are still attached to us and are drawing our energy away from our healing. If there is someone you need to forgive, take time whenever you can to do the following exercise.

1. Close your eyes. Breathe into your heart and become aware of the slowing of your breath. Put your fingers together to stimulate the feelings of peace and calm. Find a loving moment, a time when you felt generous and peaceful.

2. When you have the peaceful memory, focus on a person you need to forgive. Imagine you are attached by a cord.

3. Send your love and compassion out to this person from your heart. Watch it flowing down the cord as you say, "I forgive and release you."

4. See the cord release from your body. Watch it float away and know that you have let this person, and the resentment you felt, go and they are no longer draining your energy.

5. You can visualize any number of people in this way— many are attached to us not only by love but by sadness, anger, betrayal, grief, and so many other emotional memories. We can let them all go, leaving us—and them—to live complete lives.

We are doing amazing work here, and each chapter has been packed with suggestions and exercises that would be a lot to do under ordinary circumstances. When we're grieving, a loss of energy can be very problematic. Again, remember to be gentle with yourself; go slowly, and do only that which you feel you can handle at any one time. As for accepting all that comes, we can sit and do that with an open heart, argue vigorously, or decide that we're not ready to accept what is quite yet. All are valid and part of your healing. Your truth is what matters.

Being True to Your Core Values

We are going to continue to focus on moving beyond some of the things we have learned from authority figures in our lives, including individuals and organizations that helped us create the vision with which we see our humanity. You may find that most of what you learned in early childhood and on has served you well and created a platform for you that is solid. Others will acknowledge that some (or all) of what they have learned has been detrimental to their spiritual growth. For most of us, it is a combination of the two, and our goal here is to find those things that are not supportive and transform them. Finding our way through grief requires the strongest spiritual tools. Our core values—not other people's opinions—will support us as we move forward. And this self-awareness is one of our gifts of grief.

A Gift

We become more self-aware through our grief.

First, it is important to accept that there is no blame attached to those who taught us only what they knew. Hopefully the forgiveness exercise helped in this area. If someone comes up, it may be time to do forgiveness work with that person.

Second, we need to have enough time, at least half an hour each time we work on this process, to really look at what our basic core values are and where they came from.

We may be familiar with the idea of core values through business, where executives do visioning processes to discover the core values of their business model and their products. On a personal level, core values are the things in our lives that we live from that are nonnegotiable. They are the things we know in our hearts and live passionately, both in our personal and business lives. Our core values are at the heart of who we are, and they need to resonate with our heart's energy. If they don't, they are not our values but belong to someone else. These values are our strength, and they will get us through the darkest valleys we will face and lift us up our brightest mountains.

For example, one of my core values is to live from love. Another is to create my life's work to help others. A third, and very important, value is that I believe in telling the truth—

especially when not doing so goes against my beliefs. It literally hurts when I stuff down my sadness in order to make others feel more comfortable.

These core values developed through my love and devotion to the Blessed Mother when I was a young girl, though I never named them. As a young person, these core values were limited. Through the church and my disciplined upbringing, one person was left out of my core value of love—me. I learned from my church and my father's family that love was giving and supporting blindly, following the teachings of my church, my society, my school, and my parents. There was no room for loving dissension or addressing the doubts that I felt in my heart and gut through this particular lens of love.

When One of Your Core Values Is Put to the Test

As the upheavals of the 1960s began, I was in agonizing disagreement with the lack of progress on civil rights in the United States. Where did my devotion to love begin and end, particularly since I was an ardent believer in the words of Jesus about loving everyone? Where did my devotion to helping others begin and end under that same belief system? I felt certain that love was meant to be all-inclusive as Jesus taught, not limited as my family, church, and society taught.

In the 1970s, a private club near where I lived had an unwritten racial rule that people of color were only welcome as servers, kitchen help, or maids. The athletic staff of a university was invited to participate in a golf tournament there, which included a luncheon in the club. Imagine the consternation when one of the coaches turned out to be black. The club found a solution. Hot dogs and such were served on the course at the ninth hole, relieving everyone of the issue.

Later, I was to attend a party at that same club, hosted by a public professional organization. Given the situation I learned about, I felt it was wrong for that organization to have its meeting/party at this club. I decided to take a stand and not attend. Now that I was aware of the values of the club, going there felt like giving my approval. My decision left my husband in an uncomfortable situation. I knew this would create bad feelings among those who had breathed a sigh of relief that a confrontation had been averted during the golf tournament. I knew that my partner would find my standing on principle inconvenient and even embarrassing. Within the scope of love, causing pain to my partner created pain in me. Yet each time I considered flying under the radar and not expressing how I felt, my heart contracted and my stomach hurt. My husband's feelings were important, but my core was more important—to me. I didn't go on the radio or to the newspapers to expose the club, but if someone asked why I didn't attend the party, I told them the truth.

Since our core values are nonnegotiable, our body/heart will react anytime we are tested. If we do something that is against a core value, it will show itself to us. Then we have the choice to pay attention or ignore it. The most difficult part of being true to any core value is that it asks us to tell our truth, and we cannot deny it without paying a spiritual price. It is never a good thing to override a core value to save someone else from discomfort. They will have to address why they feel what they feel, based on their own core values.

> **The most difficult part of being true to any core value is that it asks us to tell our truth, and we cannot deny it without paying a spiritual price.**

It's not possible to bypass a core value without feeling it in the body. If you remember what it felt like to lie as a child, there were always body consequences, and you discovered the body consequences of anger through grief work. So I'm going to ask you to visit a few old power figures just to see what hold those ideas have in your life today. The great thing is, some of them will be really good models. And for those who may not be, that can be changed.

Identify the person/people/organizations your core values came from and realize that they are human and so are you, but you are a human who is beginning to know who you are. You are becoming intimate with yourself through the softening aspects of sadness and grief. You will find this to be one of the biggest gifts you will recover in this process.

Your core values can change over time, or move around in order of importance. That's natural as we grow into our soul natures. Whenever we have a decision to make, running it by our core values to see how it fits is a great way to get feedback from our heart and body.

A Gift

You are becoming intimate with yourself through the softening aspects of sadness and grief—this is one of the biggest gifts you will recover in this process.

If naming is a problem, here are some examples of words core values are built around:

+ Integrity
+ Truth
+ Family
+ Justice
+ Authenticity
+ Love

- Friendship
- Gratitude
- Loyalty
- Compassion
- Giving

Stating the words alone works for some. Stating them in an active way works best for others. There is no right or wrong way. Here are a couple of examples.

- I stand firm in my integrity no matter the challenge.
- I always place truth above convenience.
- Family will always hold a central place in my life.
- I will express gratitude in every situation.

Take a deep breath, complete the exercise, and take some time before you come back to this work.

Grief Work: Exercise 13

Uncovering Your Core Values

1. Have your journal and a pen at hand. Close your eyes and go to your heart, as you have learned. Breathe in and out slowly, feeling peace and calm come over your entire body.

2. Ask your guides and allies to form a ring of protection around you and to help you see the answers to the questions you will ask. When you feel comfortable and protected, open your eyes and answer the following questions:

- What are your top five core values? (These will be ways you desire to live your life that are filled with passion, are unquestionable, and cannot be compromised.) Write them in your journal.

- To be sure that these are truly your core values, say each value out loud and see how it resonates in your body. You can tell if there is no passion when you write or say the value out loud.

- If you did have a value or two fall flat, is it possible you're just saying what others think you should say? Might the value be from old beliefs and need to be updated? Are you ready to let go of those which no longer serve you? Adjust your core value list as necessary.

- How do you express each of these values in your daily life?

- What can you do to make your core values more energetically alive in your life?

You will want to revisit this list often in the next month or so, refining it as you go.

It is truly essential that this chapter become a part of your healing, thus a part of your being. Those power figures of your childhood or in your schools, or in your life as a partner, parent, or organization, have had their say. You are now able to look through your energetic body, your intellect, and especially your heart and know what parts of the old system are no longer useful to the you that is emerging. We are not trying to prove these people or experiences are wrong; rather, we want to accept that we have been given the gifts of love, perception, and guidance that cannot be overcome by someone else's opinion or dogma.

Our challenge is to leave the past and focus on the present. Though we'll revisit the past often with the help of the work we are doing, those visits will become less and less painful and more mindful.

A Gift
Becoming mindful of our perception and guidance is a gift we should cherish daily.

We can also visit past power figures in our protected meditations and thank them for whatever tools they gave us that we are keeping, and then move on and away from others that are no longer useful. The focus is moving from the authority and orders of other people and institutions into the knowingness supplied by our hearts, minds, and energies. Meditating on our core values and the certainties provided through these values and our own inner guidance is simple, free, and always at our fingertips.

The focus is moving from the authority and orders of other people and institutions into the knowingness supplied by our hearts, minds, and energies.

Some people lose their way for years trying to *get* a dogma. I am clear that I have no desire to be anyone's guru—my path on this earth is to help people find their own direction in life through their heart and soul. My way is not necessarily your way, and yet there are some clear and grounded similarities on the path. Structure and rules comfort the mind and we give over to what we see as a greater authority. The solution is that your soul already knows who and what you are spiritually and emotionally. Going there, going through the heart and through the messiness of love and loss, is the gift we've been given as humans.

What I am showing you is a way to yourself—to your own unfailing guidance—that I learned when I turned off the noise of earlier people or institutions to whom I had given my own power.

Whatever you choose to call your origins—God, the Universe, your Higher Power—you are now certain that you came here with the ability to know what is right, just, and loving for you. Go frequently to your core values and your all-knowing guidance, and your journey through grief will have purpose and value. You are not trading one dogma for another—my belief is in you and your heart's intelligence. You are not saying you are better—you are saying you are able. With faith in your core values and inner guidance, you will continue to create your life in the image of the gifts you've found within your grieving.

Chapter 7

Setbacks and Looking to the Future

The more you sense the rareness and value of your own life, the more you realize that how you use it, how you manifest it, is all your responsibility. We face such a big task, so naturally we sit down for a while.

—Kobun Chino Otogawa Roshi

There comes a time on the long road through grieving when we are tired and simply want to lay our burdens down. Like the journey through Dr. Kübler-Ross's five stages of grief—denial, anger, bargaining, depression, and acceptance—we have gone forward, backward, and sideways, making progress, losing momentum, and eventually, at some point, there will be a full stop. If this is happening, it's time for a rest period.

The first sections of this book have asked a lot. (I know it is a lot because I've been there, and there were times I wanted to say "Enough!" These were the times when I was just about to turn a corner on coming out of the fog.) Some of what I've asked you to do has been deep and introspective, some has asked that you embrace the process of learning to listen to your body—especially your heart-brain and your energetic field. All of the knowing, practicing, and reinventing has acknowledged that we have capacities we haven't even begun to tap into. Yet, our energy for the journey through grief is low right now, sapped by our emotional attachments to what has happened.

Remember, our grief and our struggles make us who we are. But there is no timeline that you have to adhere to—there's no deadline we need to meet to get to the finish line. This is a good time to rest, review, and reimagine the rest of the journey. If you're at the point where prayer becomes impossible, know that your body and soul are asking you to take a break, and that is what's best for your healing. The next step will be revealed once we have a chance to step back, refresh, and see the whole picture.

To begin the process of "cocooning," which is what I call this resting process, it helps to go into meditation—or simple daydreaming—and ask our guides and our higher self to fill us with peace. From within that peace and restorative place we will envision the next step on our journey.

Move at Your Own Speed

The ways the world sees grief may not acknowledge what you are going through, and sometimes even our families and friends are less than supportive. Their advice kicks in after the frustration of hearing you tell your story once too often. This is especially true with issues like divorce. "Move on!" they beg. "Get over it. There are lots of fish in the pond. Dye your hair, have an eye lift. You'll feel better."

Most of the people you're close to won't say things like this, at least in the beginning, following a *real* death. They will grant you a grace period to begin to get over these types of grief because death is the biggest fear of most people. They will feel it with you because they love you, of course, but also because it feeds into their fear. "It could happen to me," they think, and they will pray for protection. Actual death is the unthinkable. We see this in the ways death and dying are presented in the United States—behind closed doors, inside satin caskets, clean and neat and covered with make-up and flowers. Even in the graveyard, a bright green rug covers the grave so we won't see the hole in the earth. It is a denial that is not understandable in other cultures.

I remember Deepak Chopra telling the touching story of how he bathed his father's body after his death and carried him through the streets to the place where he would be burned.

After he laid his father on the burning pyre, he saw a small child flying a kite in the updraft created by the flames. To him, the boy was an illustration of living and dying being intimately connected in the cycle of life. Knowing that *everyone* dies, how do we manage to live life thinking it won't happen to us?

Eventually, in our fast-paced world, even friends will wonder why we're not moving on. Most grieving people return to their original feelings on the anniversary of the death, loss, or divorce, or the date of a birthday or marriage. A holiday continues to be a trigger for a very long time—even a lifetime. Some people will actually say, "Aren't you over that yet? It's been five years!" It is our heart that remembers and wishes to recognize our experience.

When a loved one dies unexpectedly, the process is even more dramatic—especially if the death is of a spouse, a child, or a young person. We're not given any time to pre-grieve, as we would with a long illness or decline.

Intuition

Eyes see only light, ears hear only sound, but a listening heart perceives meaning.

—David Steindl-Rast, *A Listening Heart*

Our intuition becomes paramount when we are hanging in that dark space between caterpillar and butterfly. It's the perfect time to enter the silence and listen to our higher guidance. Intuition is the soul talking to us *through* our higher self. With all the chatter flowing through our heads, we must find ways to listen to our intuition.

As we've gone through some of the grief processes, I've recommended ways to see thoughts and let them go. However, if they're just replaced by other repetitive thoughts, we are still not tuning in to the power of our intuitive self. Only through practice can we begin to see that we are guided by our higher self on a minute-by-minute basis. Meditation, prayer, heart focus, and contemplation are all different names for ways of being in the moment—which quiets the mind—and are the only ways to hear the important messages we're receiving through the heart and soul.

Sometimes becoming aware of our intuition—our heart/soul messages—is as simple as suddenly deciding to take a different route to work. We'll shrug and say we just needed variety, but usually it's our intuition warning us to avoid our usual way. If we're lucky, we may hear later that the traffic was backed up for miles on our usual route or some other confirmation that tells us our intuition has been operating.

A Gift

Rediscovering our intuition, that innate knowledge we had as children, is a pearl beyond price.

Our intuition comes from a higher place and needs our attention. Only through quieting the mind can we hear and choose to react. Our intuition and knowing step into our lives on a regular basis. And it is important that we acknowledge the presence of more than we understand and seek to strengthen our connection to a place of peace and knowledge. Simply being aware of our body's energy field and its connection to other energy fields is enough to begin.

The intuitive part of our life will be strengthened by this awareness of our body's energy and its connection to all other energy. Meditative and focused techniques allow us to provide a quiet space for our intuition and connection to our higher self to come to the forefront. We thrive if we use these techniques while we're in a time of cocooning consciously. However, being forced into a period of bed rest through illness is often the only way our higher self can get our attention. I recommend that we avoid this strategy and make a conscious choice for listening to those things we rarely hear.

When I was in a space of busyness and productivity and refused to enter into the heavy darkness of my grief, I had one illness after another—one so filled with chronic pain that all my thoughts were focused inward. But then, after healing, I went back to busyness as usual. Eventually a severe accident put me in bed for weeks. I began to read, write, and meditate and entered my dark night of the soul fully. Though I begged to be spared the full impact of my grieving, I had received a gift from the part of me that knew more than I knew consciously. It was a fact that if I kept on as I was, I would cease to function consciously.

When my exhaustion didn't ground me, an accident did. It was in that bed of pain at that particular time that I came face to face with myself and made a promise to fulfill my life as it was meant to be.

My love for my son was not to be turned into an unlived life. Slowly I began to heal. My books, workshops, and working one on one with people in grief would never have happened without that time of cocooning. Without learning to value my life, I wouldn't have been free, or able, to value the life of others. I began to see the arc of my son's life, and his contributions, and I found joy again. The same will happen for you.

The most important thing we have been learning in our journey through grief is the value of our own life. We are learning to be aware of our heart's messages, the beauty amid the darkness, and the gift of the remainder of our time on this Earth as we mourn the losses that have caused us grief.

A Gift

Grief takes us back to the basics: we recognize that life is finite, though energy is not. If we let it, this knowing will change the way we live in the moment.

Denial, anger, and exhaustion are often the results of big spiritual work and the efforts to change our perspective. We can sit down for a while. We don't have to go out and tell the world what we've learned and judge ourselves every time we don't live up to our new expectations or what we think is expected of us. We just need to sit in our new knowledge, heal, and wait. And in that waiting, we can ask for guidance to put into effect later.

I am reminded of a saying from the Talmud that is all you need to know to stand firm in your intentions:

Do not be daunted by the enormity of the world's grief. Do justly, now. Love mercy, now. Walk humbly, now. You are not obligated to complete the work, but neither are you free to abandon it.

I don't read "but neither are you free to abandon it" as a warning. Throughout my life as a teacher, a friend, and a provider of a listening ear and counseling heart, I have never seen anyone walk away from the work of healing without the nagging sense that they still have work to do. They may say it's too hard or they are finished, but daily, and sometimes nightly in their dreams, they are nudged and whispered to by their higher self and their guides. They know there is work they have to do on this planet and unless they do it, they will not live their optimal possibilities.

Through grief's vulnerabilities, we have the opportunity to recognize our true human and spiritual selves. We have been given the chance to grow, change, and become more aware of the world around us. Contrary to what much poetry and many books might tell us, this is not a slow, comfortable, or lovely process; it is wrenching, explosive, and overwhelming.

The amazing writer, suffragette, and Jungian analyst Florida Scott-Maxwell suffered deep grief in her life, and particularly in old age. She sums up this process in her book *The Measure of My Days*: "Life does not accommodate you, it shatters you. . . . Every seed destroys its container or else there would be no fruition."

Fruition is what we are seeking, it is the grail we are hunting for on our hero's quest. We hope that as we look back on our lives, we will see our grief as a path to something other than despair. Yes, it takes effort, pain, and that shattering Scott-Maxwell refers to. Yet I promise you, the results are equal to the effort. The person we will be bears a resemblance to our former self, but is deeper, stronger, and more aware of the suffering of others. Our hearts expand to include all we were unaware of before our visitation. We soften the experience through our bodywork, especially meditation, but how we got here does not change.

A Gift
Our hearts and souls expand as we walk the path of grief.

Tools for Living a Sacred Life

There are a few things we can do to encourage our souls to be heard through our heart. Many of the visualizations you learned earlier are helpful in that way. We don't live lives of isolation or hang out up on the mountain in a cave, though that would probably make the process a lot easier. We are humans learning to blend our daily life with our spiritual life while living in our busy, noisy universe. We must carve out what we need for both to blend. Here are some of the useful tools I learned on my journey.

Find Some Silence Every Day

Whatever our lives are like, we have to find ways to create our moments of silence where our contemplation will bear fruit. For me, having television and radio-free zones where I can go to be alone with my spirit is key. If you're a parent, explain that you need time in your space—usually the bedroom or going for a walk in nature—where conversation and noise are not welcome. Those who love you will understand and even help you to find what you need. Those who protest and demand your attention have issues that are not yours. If you have children, they will learn by your example what will help them as they grow into teens and adults. Be firm.

Find silence in your spaces at least twice a day. If you're at work, you might have to say you're working on a project (which you are!). Hang up a "do not disturb" sign. If you have family living with you, or roommates, have a heart-to-heart talk with them about why you need quiet time. People worry that when we're alone we're suffering, and they want to make it better by being with us. Be clear—it's not about them. It's what *we* need.

Notice Your Breath

Practice noticing your breathing throughout the day; when your focus is on your breath, you're not thinking about other things. Bring it to your heart if it's high in your chest. Slow it down. Breathe. Ask, "Where are my shoulders?" Notice, relax them if they're tight, and keep on going. It takes only a few seconds each time.

Practice prayer, contemplation, or meditation before getting up and just before bed. Learn to see these as opportunities to be grateful and express love rather than chances to ask for something.

Show Gratitude

Barn's burnt down—

now

I can see the moon.

—Mizuta Masahide

The most important tool, and the easiest, is to feel and express gratitude. Consciously notice throughout the day what you appreciate. If someone in your world does something you notice and are grateful for, tell them. Expressing it makes it become more real in your body. Gradually appreciation and gratitude will replace judgment and resentment. It's worth repeating the quote each day that we learned earlier from A Course in Miracles:

Every decision I make is a choice between a grievance and a miracle.

I relinquish all regrets, grievances and resentments and I choose the miracle.

Come back to this whenever you need to make a decision or when something happens that challenges your ability to be nonjudgmental or compassionate.

Consciously notice throughout the day what you appreciate. Expressing it makes it become more real in your body.

The average human being has a thousand thoughts an *hour*. Anything that stops the useless chatter helps us to focus on the important hints and intuitions that are trying to get through. Gratitude is one way to not only stop the mind's ruminations but to go into our heart space instantly. We don't start with the big things, as Masahide points out in his oft-quoted haiku on the previous page.

In our world, when people say we should be grateful for what we have left, we are spiritually aware that we must first go through the process of grieving. Otherwise it feels like a false gratitude. Once we are well on the journey, we can take small steps of gratitude to strengthen our hearts and help us along the way. Begin by being grateful before you open your eyes in the morning, even if you're only grateful that you can open your eyes. As you go throughout your day, find other examples of gratitude, especially within nature or among those who love and care for you. Ralph Waldo Emerson recorded this advice: "Never lose an opportunity of seeing anything that is beautiful; for beauty is God's handwriting—a wayside sacrament. Welcome it in every fair face, in every fair sky, in every fair flower, and thank God for it as a cup of blessing."

When you notice love, peace, or beauty in even small places in your life, record these examples in your journal as often as you can. You'll be building a reservoir of gratefulness. When you are healing and using your heart tools regularly, you might decide to start a separate journal called a Gratitude Journal. Many people find this to be an amazing tool for their energetic life, underpinning all of their other practices.

Grief Work: Exercise 14

Gratitude

As always, I hope you have your journal nearby and the MP3 or your music. Wait until you have quiet time, usually first thing in the morning or before bed or if you wake during the night. This process requires your concentration and that you not be interrupted.

1. Put your feet flat on the floor and close your eyes. As you settle in, begin to breathe in deeply, slowly, and gently, counting to five slowly on the inhale and five slowly on the exhale. Imagine that you are breathing into your heart. Take your time and just breathe deeply, in and out, through and around your heart.

2. As you breathe, ask any of your allies in spirit to join and support you as you work. Breathe.

3. Now see a gentle color tinting the air going in and out

of your chest. See it filtering through your lungs as you breathe in and filtering through your heart as you breathe out. Breathe.

4. As you continue focusing on your breath, infuse that colored breath with gratitude. Think of something in your life that you are grateful for as you continue to breathe in and out, slowly. It doesn't have to be a big thing—you can be grateful that your legs work and you were able to go for a walk; or that your eyes work and you were able to see a tree or a bird today; or just grateful that you are breathing deeply. Breathe. Breathe in gratitude.

5. Now bathe your heart and lungs in this feeling of gratitude. Just think of your gratitude as a flowing in and out. Be grateful that though your heart is wounded, it still pumps your lifeblood and notices where you are in your life.

6. Now lift that gratitude up—breathe it into your whole chest, your neck, your head, then down into your shoulders, arms, and hands. Imagine your whole upper body is filled with this beautiful colored light and feelings of gratitude. Tell your body how grateful you are for its ability to work for you and protect you.

7. Slowly, gently, watch this color and gratitude wash down into your lower body, through your pelvis, your legs, your ankles, and feet, and then bring it back up, slowly, until it settles around your heart. Breathe deeply, and watch as the color slowly fades and your attention comes back to your surroundings.

This is a healing process that you can do as many times as you'd like, as long as you're comfortable. Soon it will become second nature to notice your gratitude. When you're ready, open your eyes and write in your journal, noting what it feels like to appreciate your own body.

We can see by the next poem that Rumi has core values of gratitude and acceptance. He greeted each day of his life in the same way, whether it was filled with sorrow or joy.

The Guest House

This being human is a guest house.
Every morning a new arrival.

A joy, a depression, a meanness,
some momentary awareness comes
as an unexpected visitor.

Welcome and entertain them all!
Even if they're a crowd of sorrows,
who violently sweep your house
empty of its furniture,
still, treat each guest honorably.
He may be clearing you out
for some new delight.

The dark thought, the shame, the malice,

meet them at the door laughing,

and invite them in.

Be grateful for whoever comes,

because each has been sent

as a guide from beyond.

—Rumi, translated by Coleman Barks

Because Rumi's spiritual development was beyond most everyone, it was hard for people of his day to see the possibility of total acceptance as a core value. It's still a concept we struggle with even today. But when we add more gratitude into our daily meditation and journaling, we are reaching for our best self, and I'm sure Rumi would say that is enough—for now. How we grieve expresses who we are.

Sharing Your Energy with the World

As we connect to our communities and our world—and eventually the universe—we become more aware of our *real* connections. Like the systems inside our body that work together to keep us healthy and alive, we are connected to all other beings. Our feelings of gratitude, peace, and love will strengthen that connection and the health of the planet as we do this process. If you would like to feel connected with others in a more physical way,

I have included information on the Global Coherence Initiative in the resources section. This site invites people to join together in their meditations to create real energetic differences on the planet.

> **In this time of cocooning comes the opportunity to reenvision our future. One of the gifts of grief is the chance to say what we want our future to look like.**

Grief Work: Exercise 15

Sharing Your Higher Self with the World

Find a quiet time and space where you won't be interrupted. Listen to the MP3 or your own music, or let the quiet be quiet. It is always your choice.

1. Sit with your feet flat on the floor, eyes closed. If you feel more comfortable, lie down.

2. Breathe in deeply for a count of five, exhale for a count of five. Tint your breath with the color you recognize as peaceful.

3. Now breathe in through your heart, seeing the colored breath bathing your heart space, filling your chest.

The Gifts of Grief

4. On the exhale, drop the breath into your abdomen and breathe out, seeing the breath flowing outward from your abdomen. Continue inhaling through the heart and exhaling through the abdomen.

5. Begin to add the emotions of love and peace to the colored breath as it flows into your heart. See love and peace flowing out of your abdomen and into the space around you, into your home, your community, the world. Keep breathing for a few minutes. Breathe in love and peace, breathe out love and peace.

6. Now watch as the beautiful breath of love and peace comes back into your body. As you inhale, wash this beautiful breath from your heart throughout your whole body. See it flow down into your feet on the inhale, then up and out the top of your head on the exhale. Do this several times. Breathe in deeply, breathe out deeply.

7. Focus your breath back to your heart and watch it rise up through your throat until it is above your head. Let it hover just above your head and watch as the color of the breath becomes deeper and deeper and begins to shimmer. This is the location of your higher self, the connection between you and your soul's desires for you. Watch. Breathe.

8. Ask for a message or feeling from your higher self, particularly about what is most difficult for you in your life and your grieving right now. Listen carefully as you breathe deeply through your heart, up to your higher self, and back into your heart. Do this for a few minutes. If you are receiving a message or emotional information, continue this part of the process as long as you feel that's happening. Breathe.

9. When you're ready, bring your breath back to the heart. Breathe deeply in and out of your heart and gradually watch as the color begins to fade. Relax your whole body and express gratitude for being shown the connection between you and the world of your higher self. Breathe.

Write what this exercise felt like in your journal. What information or feelings did you receive? Repeat this exercise when you know you won't be disturbed. It will become more powerful as it becomes more familiar.

Review Your Progress So Far

Looking into the future is a strong process, but we must begin only after we have addressed the past. We've spent a lot of time looking into our heart, seeking out our grief in order to heal it. We have now entered the resting phase where it is our labor of self-love to take all we've learned into our hearts and heal our wounds. You have done an enormous amount up to this point. Now may be a good time to go back and reflect. You may want to review the notes in your journal and revisit the exercises.

There is a huge world awaiting you—a world where you have renewed your promises to yourself and reawakened the world you want to inhabit. Getting the breathing and heart-based exercises to become an integral part of your day is your major task right now. The gifts of peace that come from these processes will serve you the rest of your life.

There is a huge world awaiting you—a world where you have renewed your promises to yourself and reawakened the world you want to inhabit.

There is one more process that we began earlier—listening to our heart. In chapter 1, we went to the heart to see its wounding and ask what it needed to heal. Now, if you're ready, it's time to go back to those visualizations and ask the same questions and see how far you have come. If you've made notes in your journal, it will be helpful to compare notes after you redo the exercises. Do this whenever you feel you have the time, space, and quiet to really be with the process and see what is still needed to heal your heart. The heart will tell you, either through words, symbols, or simply an intuition of what's happening. Take time and be patient with yourself. I'm certain you have found greater patience after all this practice.

The Future

In this time of cocooning comes the opportunity to reenvision our future.

A Gift
Grief gives us the chance to say what we want our future to look like.

One of the gifts of grief is the chance to say what we want our future to look like.

It's as if we have a before and after time—I call mine Before Michael and After Michael. We are journeying through the grieving process and will find that our world will be totally different whether we have any say in it or not. It's essential that we make a conscious choice. We have an opportunity to see through the lens of our grief and let go of those things we thought were so important before our journey, but those now seem superfluous. It's as if we discover we're going on a backpacking trip when we'd packed a trunk for a cruise to Europe. We need to remove all those things that are unnecessary and keep only those that matter to our survival.

While you're retreating into the silence, take the following series of questions with you. Each time you look at the list, go to your heart and your guidance and ask for truth and clarity. Write about your feelings in your journal as you answer the questions. Do this when you feel you'll have at least fifteen minutes, and hopefully you'll have more time than that. Explore your answers deeply, leaving behind all training that tells you to overlook your feelings in order to be "nice." You are doing deep truth work here. Your answers may change as you figure new things out, so be sure to revisit this list once every couple of weeks.

- Before you began this process, what people and things were most important to you?

- As you near the end of the book (though not the grieving process), have any of these people or things become less important?

- Are there people who you find are uncomfortable or less important in your life based on who you have become? Who has become more important? Can you say why?

- Has any one thing become more important as you apply the lessons of peace, love, and gratitude?

- Are there new objectives or perspectives that you want to apply to your life right now? Be as specific as you can.

- Are there any gifts that you can now say you've received or uncovered?

- Have your core values changed or remained the same? If the same, have they strengthened through the grieving process?

- Has your ability to meditate, pray, or contemplate strengthened on this journey?

- How has your breathing changed?

Based on the answers to these questions, you may feel that there are one or two areas where you want to focus more of your attention as you return to the work. Right now, we are looking at the progress we've made, resting in the meditations, and projecting a bit into the future by imagining what our world will look like as we apply the lessons of the journey through grief.

It's important to write about your experience doing this exercise in your journal so that when you do it again, you can see any changes or strengthening of certain parts. As it is with your core values, your higher self will begin to help you sort your desires and feelings about your future. Come back to this as often as possible when you are in your resting stage and begin with noticing your breath.

Grief Work: Exercise 16

Looking Ahead

Find a time when you will be undisturbed and quiet. Listen to the MP3 or your favorite music if you wish.

1. Sit with your feet flat on the floor, or lie down if that's better for you, and begin to breathe slowly and quietly into and out of your heart.

2. Imagine your body rising slowly and floating above your chair or bed. You are using your imagination, so you are safe. As you are floating, imagine a beautiful path beneath you, with white stone, packed dirt, sand, brick— whatever you like. The path could be winding through the woods, along a river, along the seashore, or through a beautiful garden. This path is your life journey. You are in the present, part of the path is in the past behind you, and part of the path leads to your future. Stay here for a

moment, envisioning what the path in front of you looks like as your future. Breathe.

3. Now gradually begin to float forward into your future, leaving your past behind you. Visualize the beauty that is possible. Imagine people and places below you that you want to be a part of your future. See light shining down on the path, illuminating places of joy and celebration. See yourself in this place, healthy, joyous, and peaceful as you look down upon you and your future. Breathe. Move along and see those things happening that are the stuff of your dreams—you receiving a diploma, writing a book, painting a picture, helping other people meet their dreams. Whatever your dream is, take your time and see this whole and real in your future. Visualize it in living color, vibrant sound, loving emotions. If it's a business you want to build, a home you want to create, a person you want to be with, a book you want to write, see it complete and whole, rising up from the path of your future. Take time to give this scene color and life. Breathe.

4. When you're ready, move along the path of your future to your old age. See yourself as you absolutely wish to be—in vibrant health, of peaceful countenance, and whole-hearted. Take your time to see, smell, or even touch all of these aspects of yourself and pay attention to how you will affect others as you advance in years. Before you finish, ask your older, wiser self if they have any words for you. Take your time and listen fully—this may be the most important part of this visualization. Breathe deeply.

5. When you have finished visiting with your older, wiser self, turn and float back to the present and down into

your chair or bed. Breathe deeply into and out of your heart, thanking your higher self for giving you this opportunity to see and project your future. Write in your journal each time you look ahead.

Possibilities

The future is not someplace we are going to, but one we are creating. The paths to it are not found but created, and the activity of creating them changes both the maker and the destination.

—John H. Schaar, *Legitimacy in the Modern State*

As our journey through grief comes to a close, we begin a new journey into our new life. We are the creators of this new life, and the lessons and gifts of our grief are our cocreators. The grief will come with us, but it has passed through the light with us and is now part of our strength. There are also many new energies and attitudes that will take us through the final steps of transforming grief into the light of our new way. Compassion, intention, choice, purpose, heart strength, intuition, and gratitude are just a few of the gifts we've been given through the journey of grief. Freedom, and possibilities, await.

Albert Camus wrote, "In the depth of winter, I finally learned that within me there lay an invincible summer." Inside our heart lies the end of the quest, the grail we have been searching for, in the form of the gifts that are awaiting us. They have been there all this time, asking for our attention. But, like Dorothy, who always had the power to return to Kansas, we can only find these gifts in our own time by finding our own allies and following our own journey.

The resilient and sacred center of the human being finds the impossible possible once we are aware of the light that shines in the heart and the intentions of the soul. This light can be found in the cracks and crevices of every broken heart.

As my final gift to you, I share the poem I wrote for my son. When I wrote this poem, created from a heart that was thawing, I recognized that I was beginning to come to life again by seeing and feeling the memories of my son.

Michael
for Miller Williams

The poet read of death, loss,
masked faces in coffins.
I tried not to listen.
His warm voice smoked around
my grief, spoke an Arkansas
Spring thaw into the cold
places of my spirit. The

ice shrouding you split
like a "tear here" tab, and I
felt you again after all
these years. Not in your coffin
or at the right hand of God,
but with your sweet smelling
infant mouth on my neck,
and, later, your bright
hair crackling from the
doorway as you flung
news of your day, fled
to baseball, swimming,
as if there wasn't time
to fit it all in.
How did you know?

We are human. How can we keep from singing? May your days be blessed and your heart express its true meaning as you journey onward. May you taste joy, again. I would be honored to hear from you about your challenges and victories.

Blessings to You, Dear Reader

The blessings that follow arose in my heart as I was meditating on how to conclude this book. It's hard to say goodbye to you, knowing that I may have failed to write something that would have made your path easier. I know it is a conundrum most writers face: Am I finished? And then I heard these words come into my heart and I felt so blessed. These are from me, to you, in the hope that I have been able to illuminate the path through grief that you are traversing.

May every second be a time to feel the beat of your heart and your desire to live moment to moment.

May every minute be an opportunity to take a deep breath and feel peace.

May each day bring you closer to your center, nearer to your joy.

May each week reveal your path in a new way through love and opportunities.

May each month surprise you with the movement that has gone on in your life and the progress you have made toward being your whole beautiful self.

May each year take you further from grief and deeper into gratitude for the gifts that will last a lifetime.

—Therèse

Afterword

Follow-Up Questions

Now that you've completed your journey through this book, please revisit where you are emotionally now versus when you began. On a scale of 1–10, with 10 being the strongest and 1 being the weakest, rank how strong each of these emotions is. Breathe deeply, go to your heart for the true answers, and circle the number. Feel free to compare these answers to the answers you gave at the beginning of the book.

After Reading *The Gifts of Grief*

	Emotions/Body	Rank									
1	Sadness	1	2	3	4	5	6	7	8	9	10
2	Anger	1	2	3	4	5	6	7	8	9	10
3	Resentment	1	2	3	4	5	6	7	8	9	10
4	Lack of energy	1	2	3	4	5	6	7	8	9	10
5	Loss of interest in life	1	2	3	4	5	6	7	8	9	10
6	Gratitude	1	2	3	4	5	6	7	8	9	10
7	Hope	1	2	3	4	5	6	7	8	9	10
8	Breathing skills	1	2	3	4	5	6	7	8	9	10

If you would, please share these with me by sending them to ttappouni@aol.com.

There is always room to continue to grow and develop, and you can use the exercises presented here over and over until you feel you don't need them anymore and can just notice your breathing, breathe in love and peace, and go on about your life.

Recommended Resources

Books

Armstrong, Karen. *The Spiral Staircase: My Climb Out of Darkness*. New York: Anchor Books, 2005.

Campbell, Joseph, with Bill Moyers. *The Power of Myth*. New York: Anchor Books, 1991.

Childre, Doc, and Deborah Rozman, PhD. *Transforming Stress: The HeartMath® Solution for Relieving Worry, Fatigue, and Tension*. Oakland, CA: New Harbinger Publications, 2005.

Childre, Doc, and Howard Martin. *The HeartMath® Solution: The Institute of HeartMath's Revolutionary Program for Engaging the Power of the Heart's Intelligence*. San Francisco: HarperOne, 2000.

Chopra, Deepak. *The Path to Love: Spiritual Strategies for Healing*. New York: Three Rivers Press, 1997.

Houston, Jean, PhD. *A Passion for the Possible: A Guide to Realizing Your True Potential*. San Francisco: HarperOne, 1998.

Kübler-Ross, Elisabeth, and David Kessler. *On Grief and Grieving: Finding the Meaning of Grief through the Five Stages of Loss.* New York: Scribner, 2005.

Lewis, C. S. *A Grief Observed.* San Francisco: HarperOne, 2001.

Lipton, Bruce H., PhD. *The Biology of Belief: Unleashing the Power of Consciousness, Matter & Miracles.* Santa Cruz, CA: Mountain of Love Productions, 2005.

O'Donohue, John. *Anam Ċara: A Book of Celtic Wisdom.* New York: HarperCollins, 1998.

Tappouni, Therèse. *The Promise: Revealing the Purpose of Your Soul.* Austin, TX: Synergy Books, 2008.

Williams, Miller. *The Ways We Touch: Poems.* Urbana, IL: University of Illinois Press, 1997.

Music

2002. *Land of Forever.* Real Music B000006NYE, 1998, compact disc.

Aeoliah. *Majesty.* Oreade Music, B00004S80N, 2000, compact disc.

Hoppé, Michael, poetry by Therèse Tappouni. *Tapestry.* Spring Hill Music B00402HMAU, 2010, compact disc. Available at www.ThereseTappouni.com or IsisInstitute.org.

Hoppé, Michael, and the Prague Symphony. *Solace.* Spring Hill Music B00008PXA0, 2003, compact disc. Available at www.ThereseTappouni.com or IsisInstitute.org.

Ware, Lance. *Heart and Soul Meditations CD2: The Instrumental Version.* Living Peace Music B00005JCS9, 1999, compact disc. Available at www.ThereseTappouni.com or IsisInstitute.org.

Guided Meditation

Tappouni, Thérèse. *The Promise: Walking Your Path of Truth.* Available at www.IsisInstitute.org.

Ware, Lance. *Heart and Soul Meditations CD1: The Guided Version.* Living Peace Music, B00005JCS8, 1999, compact disc. Available through www.IsisInstitute.org.

Stress and Healing Resources

Please note that all visualizations and processes in *The Gifts of Grief* were developed and written exclusively by me. However, I give thanks and gratitude for my training in other modalities that helped me to create these processes exclusively for people who are grieving.

ThereseTappouni.com

Log on to my website, *www.theresetappouni.com,* to subscribe to my newsletter, read my blog, and purchase my products. You will also find descriptions of my work and my contact information. I welcome your ideas, suggestions, and notes on your healing.

Global Coherence Initiative (GCI)

www.glcoherence.org

The Global Coherence Initiative (GCI) is a science-based, cocreative project to unite people in heart-focused care and intention to facilitate the shift in global consciousness from instability and discord to balance, cooperation, and enduring peace. You can join at no cost to combine your energies with others to effect change, just as you did with the energy processes in the book.

HeartMath®

www.heartmath.com

For this book, I used my training as a licensed HeartMath provider to inform the breathing techniques present in my visualizations. The HeartMath Institute has many free articles and videos available on stress and what's happening in the world of science as it studies stress. For more information about the programs available, call me to book a free exploratory appointment at (727) 593-3757.

The Institute for Sacred Integrative Somatherapies (ISIS)

www.isisinstitute.org

The Institute for Sacred Integrative Somatherapies (ISIS) is the home base for work that Lance Ware and I do separately and together. We mentor clients on their path to an Intentional Life. On our website you will find additional resources. I used my training as a Somatic Intuitive Training practitioner to inform my visualizations and the process of anchoring.

About the Author

THERÈSE AMRHEIN TAPPOUNI is cofounder of the Institute for Sacred Integrative Somatherapies (ISIS) in Florida, where she and her partner help others to lead an intentional, conscious life. She is a Somatic Intuitive Training™ practitioner; a licensed HeartMath® provider; a clinical hypnotherapist; teacher, author, poet, grief counselor, and coach. Her joy is in helping others find a place in their hearts that will sustain them throughout the best and worst life has to offer.

A mother and grandmother, Tappouni has written six books and produced a CD of visualizations titled *The Promise: Walking the Path of Truth,* which accompanies her book *The Promise: Revealing the Purpose of Your Soul,* a 2008 winner of the bronze medal for women's issues from the Independent Book

Publishers Awards. Her book collaboration with her daughters, written for young children on the subject of sustainability and titled *Me and Green,* won a gold medal from the Indie Excellence Book Awards. Her latest collaboration is a book of poetry that accompanies Grammy-nominated composer Michael Hoppé's latest compositions on the CD *Tapestry.* She leads retreats and workshops for women and teaches writing.

Visit her at:
www.theresetappouni.com
www.isisinstitute.org
ttappouni@aol.com

books that inspire your body, mind, and spirit

Hierophant Publishing
8301 Broadway, Suite 219
San Antonio, TX 78209
888-800-4240

www.hierophantpublishing.com